PRAISE FOR *BUILD[...]*
MULTIETHNIC CHURCH

"Pastors listen to pastors who do pastoring well, and churches ought to listen to churches that do church well. Theory sounds better on paper more often than it works, but churches that have learned how to be the church in a fast-changing America deserve our ear. Transformation Church in Charlotte and their courageous leader, Derwin Gray, deserve our ear for one reason: they are mapping the path that leads to the multiethnic church, to a high-definition vision of what the church must become in an America increasingly filled with racial tension. Both Derwin's story and Transformation Church's are visions of a new kind of church. No vision is more needed in the United States of America because if our churches don't become multiethnic, the word *united* at the federal level will be mocked by the word *divided* in the churches. Derwin Gray has a better idea: let local churches lead by becoming united churches as a prophetic voice for a more united nation."

—SCOT MCKNIGHT, JULIUS R. MANTEY PROFESSOR
IN NEW TESTAMENT AT NORTHERN SEMINARY

"Derwin Gray is one of the leaders of an emerging army of men and women who are taking courageous steps of faith to lead, live out, and model the visible unity of the body of Christ. Anchored in God's Word, *Building a Multiethnic Church* is a compelling, prophetic call to be and look like God's church. Derwin writes not from mere observation and analysis but from engaging credibility. The church he leads is a portrait of the power of the gospel to make us one. Thank you, Derwin, for equipping us and calling us to go beyond a 'convenient success' to giving ourselves to God's holy, noble vision for his church."

—DR. CRAWFORD W. LORITTS JR., AUTHOR, SPEAKER, RADIO
HOST, AND SENIOR PASTOR OF FELLOWSHIP BIBLE CHURCH

"Derwin Gray is a provocative preacher, but an even greater visionary. He has seen what the church of tomorrow must be—indeed, what it should have been all along. This is no high-minded book about theory. He has built what he is calling the rest of us to. If we ignore the truths of this book, we do so at our peril."

—J. D. GREER, PhD, PRESIDENT OF THE SOUTHERN BAPTIST CONVENTION AND AUTHOR OF *GAINING BY LOSING* AND *WHAT ARE YOU GOING TO DO WITH YOUR LIFE?*

"This book spoke to my soul. Theologically robust. Prophetic. Passionate. *Building a Multiethnic Church* will be must-read material for the young leaders I train who have the Christ-exalting, redemptive impatience to lead multiethnic churches."

—BRYAN LORITTS, PRESIDENT OF THE KAINOS MOVEMENT AND AUTHOR OF *RIGHT COLOR, WRONG CULTURE*

"Building and being a part of a church on earth that looks and worships like the Church in heaven is a consuming passion of mine. It is also a consuming passion of my friend Derwin Gray. This book fleshes out that passion in a way that will bless, convict, instruct, and motivate. I don't think you can remain the same after reading it! So jump in and prepare to be transformed for the glory of God and the good of others."

—DANIEL L. AKIN, PRESIDENT OF SOUTHEASTERN BAPTIST THEOLOGICAL SEMINARY

"We live in a world of increasing complexity and division. In *Building a Multiethnic Church* Derwin Gray calls the church and its leaders to a new level of conviction and a new type of leadership. This book challenges convention and challenges the reader to abandon the status quo and embrace a glorious picture of ethnic unity that is made possible only in Christ. This book is a must-read."

—ED STETZER, PROFESSOR, AUTHOR, SPEAKER, AND CHURCH PLANTER

"Every so often a book comes around that changes the course of the Church by merging strong, theological principles, intelligent thought, and authentic Christ-like compassion. Gray's *Building a Multiethnic Church* is that book for the modern-day believer, leader, and pastor. Written to invoke the passion and DNA of the early church in the heart of those who forge ahead with the mission of grace and faith today, this book will birth a new zeal in us to build a Church that reflects the corridors of heaven. Get ready for a book that will magnify His call *in* you and *through* you!"

—SERGIO DE LA MORA, LEAD PASTOR OF CORNERSTONE CHURCH
OF SAN DIEGO AND AUTHOR OF *THE HEART REVOLUTION*
AND *PARADOX: THE GOD WHO BREAKS THE RULES*

"More than a half-century has passed since Martin Luther King Jr. called 11:00 a.m. on Sunday 'the most segregated hour in this nation,' and his words are still true. For shame. A racially segregated church not only fails to reflect the increasingly multiethnic make-up of America, but it also fails to live up to the biblical vision of God's kingdom. Where is this community comprised of 'every nation and tribe and people and language' that the Apostle John spoke about? But despair not, dear readers. In a moment where the church lags painfully behind the progress of society, Derwin Gray offers a clarion call for a revolution in our ranks. *Building a Multiethnic Church* arrives at the right moment and comes at you like a rocket—with superb precision and paradigm-exploding power. Skip it at your peril."

—JONATHAN MERRITT, AUTHOR OF *JESUS IS BETTER THAN YOU
IMAGINED* AND *LEARNING TO SPEAK GOD FROM SCRATCH*

"In a time when too many pastors and too many churches are content to minister among those who look like them, we need leaders with gospel courage and a biblical insight to call us out of monochromatic apathy. Derwin Gray is the right voice at the right time. Read *Building a Multiethnic Church* and be energized to see the kingdom of Christ in all its vivid diversity once again."

—DR. RUSSELL MOORE, PRESIDENT OF THE ETHICS AND RELIGIOUS
LIBERTY COMMISSION OF THE SOUTHERN BAPTIST CONVENTION

"In a time when our country is marked by great diversity and great division, we need pastors who can be 'gospel-shaped leaders' as Derwin Gray calls them. These leaders are passionate about reaching across cultures and bringing reconciliation and healing. What a timely book."

—GREG SURRATT, FOUNDING PASTOR OF SEACOAST CHURCH

"Leadership, true leadership that knows the times, has a vision of where we are to go, and guides a people there, is in severe short supply. Pastor Derwin Gray is a proven leader, and he outlines in fascinating detail how to be a godly leader in a multicolored, complex world. A fascinating and vitally important book that is exactly right for the times."

—MICHAEL EMERSON, PROFESSOR AND AUTHOR OF *DIVIDED BY FAITH*

"*Building a Multiethnic Church* is a brilliant prophetic prescription for the church in today's America. Gray exposes the elephant in the room: our churches aren't diverse in a nation that is. He then tackles the all-important question of how to break the trend and lay hold of the reconciliation God so desires for his church."

—ALBERT TATE, LEAD PASTOR OF FELLOWSHIP MONROVIA

"Pastor Derwin leads with conviction because he preaches what he practices. His words are timely and must be considered if we as the Body of Christ want to steward well the gospel message entrusted to us by God. If there's anything our churches and nation are in dire need of today, it's more multiethnic-minded leaders!"

—D. A. HORTON, ASSISTANT PROFESSOR OF INTERCULTURAL STUDIES AT CALIFORNIA BAPTIST UNIVERSITY AND COAUTHOR OF *ENTER THE RING*

"I relish the opportunity to learn leadership lessons that are humble and sustain my faith. My friend Derwin Gray has written such a book. Instead of the church running for the hills when facing adversity, we would do well to learn from our African American brothers and sisters.

This book is such a gift! The leadership lessons in this book are game changers for the church. Buy yourself a copy. Then get copies for every church leader you know."

—GABE LYONS, FOUNDER OF Q AND AUTHOR
OF *THE NEXT CHRISTIANS*

"How is it that radios have moved from flat-frequencies to surround-sound, and television has catapulted from black-and-white to technicolor, but the church still wrestles with multi-frequency and gospel-shaped leadership? In *Building a Multiethnic Church* my friend Derwin Gray challenges us to catch what has always been the gospel intention—leadership that bridges divides, celebrates difference, and calls us higher."

—REV. DR. GABRIEL SALGUERO, PRESIDENT OF NATIONAL LATINO
EVANGELISM COALITION AND PASTOR OF LAMB'S CHURCH

"Let's be honest. We are living in very turbulent times filled with increasing racial tension and division. Fear, rather than love, is the norm. And yet, in this landscape, the Church often appears silent, apathetic, or paralyzed. I often hear from other leaders that they don't quite know how to navigate this fast-changing and complex world. In *Building a Multiethnic Church*, Derwin Gray has offered leaders and the larger church an important book and resource. *Building a Multiethnic Church* is biblical, theological, personal, and highly practical. We're reminded that we must engage this journey because the gospel invites us to be agents, ministers, and leaders of reconciliation."

—EUGENE CHO, PRESIDENT AND CEO OF BREAD FOR THE WORLD
AND AUTHOR OF *OVERRATED: ARE WE MORE IN LOVE WITH THE IDEA
OF CHANGING THE WORLD THAN ACTUALLY CHANGING THE WORLD?*

BUILDING A MULTIETHNIC CHURCH

BUILDING A MULTIETHNIC CHURCH

A GOSPEL VISION *of* LOVE,
GRACE, AND RECONCILIATION
IN A DIVIDED WORLD

DR. DERWIN L. GRAY

THOMAS NELSON
Since 1798

Published in Nashville, Tennessee, by Thomas Nelson. Thomas Nelson is a registered trademark of HarperCollins Christian Publishing, Inc.

Author is represented by the literary agency The Fedd Agency, Inc., P.O. Box 341973, Austin, Texas 78734.

Thomas Nelson titles may be purchased in bulk for educational, business, fundraising, or sales promotional use. For information, please e-mail SpecialMarkets@ThomasNelson.com.

Unless otherwise noted, Scripture quotations are taken from the ESV® Bible (The Holy Bible, English Standard Version®). Copyright © 2001 by Crossway, a publishing ministry of Good News Publishers. Used by permission. All rights reserved.

Scripture quotations marked KJV are taken from the King James Version. Public domain.

Scripture quotations marked NCV are taken from the New Century Version®. Copyright © 2005 by Thomas Nelson. Used by permission. All rights reserved.

Scripture quotations marked NIV are taken from The Holy Bible, New International Version®, NIV®. Copyright © 1973, 1978, 1984, 2011 by Biblica, Inc.™ Used by permission of Zondervan. All rights reserved worldwide. www.Zondervan.com. The "NIV" and "New International Version" are trademarks registered in the United States Patent and Trademark Office by Biblica, Inc.™

Scripture quotations marked NLT are taken from the Holy Bible, New Living Translation. © 1996, 2004, 2015 by Tyndale House Foundation. Used by permission of Tyndale House Publishers, Inc., Carol Stream, Illinois 60188. All rights reserved.

Any internet addresses, phone numbers, or company or product information printed in this book are offered as a resource and are not intended in any way to be or to imply an endorsement by Thomas Nelson, nor does Thomas Nelson vouch for the existence, content, or services of these sites, phone numbers, companies, or products beyond the life of this book.

Note: Some of the names and details in the stories in this book have been changed to protect anonymity.

ISBN 978-1-4002-3055-6 (eBook)
ISBN 978-1-4002-3048-8 (TP)

Library of Congress Control Number: 2014959020

Printed in the United States of America

21 22 23 24 25   LSC   10 9 8 7 6 5 4 3 2 1

About Leadership Network

Leadership Network fosters innovation movements that activate the church to greater impact. We help shape the conversations and practices of pacesetter churches in North America and around the world. The Leadership Network mind-set identifies church leaders with forward-thinking ideas—and helps them to catalyze those ideas resulting in movements that shape the church.

Together with HarperCollins Christian Publishing, the biggest name in Christian books, the NEXT imprint of Leadership Network moves ideas to implementation for leaders to take their ideas to form, substance, and reality. Placed in the hands of other church leaders, that reality begins spreading from one leader to the next . . . and to the next . . . and to the next, where that idea begins to flourish into a full-grown movement that creates a real, tangible impact in the world around it.

NEXT: A Leadership Network Resource committed to helping you grow your next idea.

NEXT
LEADERSHIP NETWORK

*To my mother, Connie Gray. As a forty-four-year-old man,
who can now see people through the lens of God's grace, I'm
thankful that my sixteen-year-old mother chose to let me live
and not to abort me, even though she was under pressure by
her school's nurse to do so. Thank you, my mom. Hey, Mom,
I bet you never imagined your little boy with a big Afro would
grow up to play professional football, pastor a church, write
books, or have a doctorate in the New Testament. You gave
me a chance at life. I will be forever grateful. I love you.*

*To the beautiful people called Transformation Church. Eleven
years ago Transformation Church was a vision on a piece
of paper, but by God's grace that vision became a dynamic,
powerful, living reality through your multicolored lives.
"Transformers," your love for Jesus and people inspire me.
Thank you for the honor of serving you on this great adventure.
These words of the apostle reflect you: "For this reason, ever
since I heard about your faith in the Lord Jesus and your love
for all God's people, I have not stopped giving thanks for you,
remembering you in my prayers" (Ephesians 1:15–16 NIV).*

CONTENTS

FOREWORD
by Matt Chandler

Revelation 7:9–10 is one of my favorite passages in the Bible. It reads in the ESV this way: "After this I looked, and behold, a great multitude that no one could number, from every nation, from all tribes and peoples and languages, standing before the throne and before the Lamb, clothed in white robes, with palm branches in their hands, and crying out with a loud voice, 'Salvation belongs to our God who sits on the throne, and to the Lamb!'" This text has become one that I quote often and ponder on consistently. We're not there yet, but we are closer than when you first picked up this book. This is really going to happen. Men and women from every background, ethnicity, and language imaginable will be gathered together to worship and praise our Savior. As a man who reverse engineers to get things done, this image is burned into my imagination as something I am to think on, pray for, and work toward now. I am convinced the multiethnic church has been purchased by Christ on the cross and is God's heart for his people. It's not the gospel and should never be elevated to that level, but it is a serious implication and benefit of the gospel . . . but how do we get there?

The truth is, I pastor a church in the middle of a predominantly White part of the Dallas/Fort Worth metroplex. Our elders grew convicted that we had not given ourselves over to pursue racial reconciliation and work toward seeing The Village look more like Revelation 7 and less like a bleached-out Mayberry in a snow storm with a couple of brown dots. For the last five to seven years, we have sought to understand theologically, philosophically, and practically what it will look like to become a "multiethnic, Christ-centered, gospel-shaped church" and have given ourselves over to that prayerful and difficult pursuit. The fruit has been stunning, and we are a more mature, more passionate, more worshipful church because of it.

I am more grateful that I can express for my brother and friend Derwin Gray. A deep zeal for Jesus can be felt just hanging around him. *Building a Multiethnic Church* is a real gift to anyone who earnestly desires to lead effectively in our world that is growing increasingly more diverse. *Building a Multiethnic Church* avoids all the pitfalls that can be present in books on multiethnic ministry. Derwin writes biblically, stays tethered to the Scriptures, captures the nuances of the gospel brilliantly, and is fearless about the doctrines that drive this issue. He faithfully shows us that multiethnic ministry was God's plan from the beginning. Many books on this subject stop there. They have their place, and I am grateful for how they shaped my understanding on this issue, but *Building a Multiethnic Church* doesn't stop there. This isn't just a theological idea book, but one rooted richly in doctrine that moves us into best practices. If you're like I am, I was compelled by the theological truth long before I knew what to do with them. Derwin dances between the theological, philosophical, and practical implications better than anyone else I have read. That's why I'm confident that wherever you find yourself on the journey toward a more multi-ethnic church, this book will serve you.

Because you are reading this, I am hopefully praying that you are a part of a new generation of "courageous pioneers" like those Derwin reminds us of in the church at Antioch. This journey won't be an easy one. There is much hurt, skepticism, and unresolved anger and pain that still affects how we view each other. You'll need to be fearless, rooted in the gospel, zealous for the fame of Jesus, and willing to lead us forward. Before Derwin takes over, take a second and read Revelation 7 again: "After this I looked, and behold, a great multitude that no one could number, from every nation, from all tribes and peoples and languages, standing before the throne and before the Lamb, clothed in white robes, with palm branches in their hands, and crying out with a loud voice, 'Salvation belongs to our God who sits on the throne, and to the Lamb!'"

Can you imagine it? We *will* get there! God always accomplishes what he purposes.

—MATT CHANDLER,
LEAD PASTOR OF THE VILLAGE CHURCH AND
PRESIDENT OF ACTS 29 CHURCH PLANTING
NETWORK

INTRODUCTION

WHAT IS A GOSPEL-SHAPED LEADER?

We need gospel-shaped leaders who can lead the church into America's multicolored future. Just as high-definition television allows one to see colors vividly, clearly, and beautifully, we need church leaders who can build multicolored local churches through the Spirit's power so America can see God's character vividly, clearly, and beautifully through his diverse people.

A leader shaped by the gospel is a leader who is so passionate about the glory of God being revealed through the local church that he or she is willing to learn how to be a cross-cultural, gospel-of-grace preaching, organizational-strategizing, leader-developing disciple of people who partners with the Lord Jesus in building local churches that reflect the future of the church in the present. (Revelation 5:9–12)

Gospel-shaped leaders learn from the apostle Paul, therefore, the book of Ephesians will be our road map, along with other selected texts. We will journey with Paul as he builds a heavenly community on earth in the local churches at Ephesus, in what is now modern-day Turkey.

Every great football coach I had held the ability to teach us the game by saying the same things in different ways. Throughout this book, I will do likewise; I will share the same gospel truths in different ways. So if you think I am repeating some things, I am! I want to drive the truths of this book deep into your heart.

In chapter 1, my goal is to shock your thought paradigm and introduce the idea of gospel-shaped leadership and why it's needed. In chapter 2, I'm going to share my journey and the unlikely story of Transformation Church. In chapter 3, we're going to look at salvation through the lens of upward, inward, and outward and explore what that means. This will increase and deepen your understanding of what Jesus actually accomplished. In chapter 4, we're going to explore God's eternal plans—seeing Jesus, his work, and what his work accomplished from a fuller, richer perspective. In chapter 5, we will look at being missional through reconciliation and what that looks like in the local church. In chapter 6, we are going to examine the term *gospel* and what it means for individuals and what it means for the local church. As you read chapter 6, you may throw away the book. You might even want to slap somebody and shout, "How did I not know this?" But I'm not presenting anything new, just the essential truth of the gospel in a different way. In chapter 7, we'll look at what it means to be the new people of God, the bride of Christ, the gospel-shaped church. In chapter 8, we'll look at discipleship and leadership developed according to a gospel vision. And in chapter 9, we'll look at what a new heaven and a new earth might look like and describe the role of the church until Jesus returns.

Pastors and leaders ask me, "What have you guys done at Transformation Church for it to become multiethnic and one of the fastest-growing churches in America?" I tell them, "That's the wrong question. Ask us who we are first. Then ask, 'How did you become like you are?' Then ask, 'What are the practices you implement to build a multiethnic church?'"

In the pages of this book you will be submerged in lots of theology. The Spirit of God has used theology to shape me and Transformation Church into who we are and into how we developed the practices to best fit our missional context. Many of our ministry practices are birthed right out of the New Testament. Many are the products of our missional context. Your context will be different from ours, but the theology will transcend and fit into any missional context. If your desire is to plant a multiethnic local church or transform a homogeneous local church into a multiethnic local church, you and your team will need to wrestle with the Holy Spirit to develop your own practices to fit where you are. However, the theology will transcend any context and will operate as your guiding principles.

Here's a letter I received from a seventy-year-old White couple in our church who've been married for fifty-one years:

Dear Pastor Derwin,

I have enjoyed your first two books and am excited about *Building Multiethnic Churches: A Gospel Vision of Love, Grace, and Reconciliation in a Divided World.*

I have actively attended and worshiped at traditional churches in America for about fifty years and am often asked why I now attend a nondenominational, multiethnic, multi-generational one that has loud contemporary music. Usually I answer, "Because people are coming to Jesus and getting baptized all of the time and lives are being transformed."

Matthew 16:18 tells us that the Rock, which is [God's] Son, is the foundation of the church, and that is the only answer to a thriving, successful church. Christ must be lifted up to draw men unto him, and a high and lofty view of God is of utmost importance. I find this to be evident in all areas at Transformation Church. It is a pleasure to worship there and helps me focus on him.

The thing that matters is that he be lifted up. When he is lifted up, not only does he draw men to himself, he draws men to each other in unity.

Because the church has been segregated for so many years, I appreciate the call to "intentionally" worship across racial and cultural lines. I know that when Jesus calls us to become like him, he means in all ways, and sometimes we don't even know what that is until we are informed and inspired by others. Each step we make to become more like him is a blessing to us.

I think the reason Transformation Church is succeeding is because it pleases God. A high and lofty view of God and a continual, strong call to follow him and his desires for us from the pulpit is what is enabling his sheep to follow.

I will pray for you as you write this new book.

Thank you for taking this journey with me. But it's not about me or you. It's about Jesus' glory, yet he uses all of me and all of you to bring forth his glory. And Jesus is most glorified when his bride, the church, reveals her beautiful, multicolored face.

ONE

GOSPEL-SHAPED LEADERSHIP

He made peace between Jews and Gentiles by creating
in himself one new people from the two groups.
Together as one body, Christ reconciled both groups
to God by means of his death on the cross, and our
hostility toward each other was put to death.
—EPHESIANS 2:15–16 NLT

THE TSUNAMI IS ON ITS WAY

Times are changing. You can feel it. You can sense something in the air. America is starting to look and feel a whole lot different. For the first time in the country's history, ethnic and racial minorities "are projected to make up the majority of students attending American public schools this fall, ending the white-majority population that has existed from the beginnings of the public education system."[1]

In 1960, the population of the United States was 85 percent

White; by 2060, it will be only 43 percent.[2] The face of America is no longer just Black and White, like those old televisions from back in the day. America is filled with different colored people. America is now a beautiful mosaic that includes Asian and Latino brothers and sisters.

Since 1965, forty million immigrants have arrived in the United States, "about half of them Hispanics and nearly three-in-ten Asians."[3] In addition, "Intermarriage is playing a big role in changing some of our views of ethnicity."[4] I know this to be true from personal experience; my wife is a White girl from rural Montana, and I'm a Black guy from urban San Antonio, Texas. We have two stunningly beautiful children. When our children are asked to fill out an ethnicity questionnaire, they write, "We are children of God who happen to have a Black father and a White mother."

Not in Mayberry Anymore

What do all of these statistics mean? They mean we no longer live in a Black or White America. We live in a beautiful, multicolored America. It means we are not in Mayberry anymore. It means that the ethnic diversity of New York City, Los Angeles, and Houston is coming to a neighborhood near you much sooner than you think. Pastor, are you and your church ready to embrace this new community, or will you futilely attempt to maintain a homogeneous ministry in a multicolored world? The church needs new kinds of leaders, cross-cultural leaders who can guide the church into a multicolored America and world. Are you that leader? For the sake of the gospel and Jesus' church and glory, I sure hope you are this leader. Or at least desire to be this kind of leader.

JUST BEFORE A TSUNAMI

Before a tsunami hits land, the water level drops as water pulls away from the shore, leaving a wide chasm and exposing the seabed. Denominational leaders, pastors, church planters, and elders of homogeneous churches, I want you to know that the seas of change have pulled back from the beach and the tsunami is coming fast. The church needs a new kind of leader who can see this sea change coming and prepare the church and God's people for it. Don't let the tsunami crush Jesus' church.

BLACKBERRY CHURCHES IN AN ANDROID/IPHONE WORLD

Blackberry used to be synonymous with the word *smartphone*. From 2000 to 2007, Blackberry phones were considered cool and were nicknamed "Crackberries" because of their addictive nature. Celebrities and Fortune 500 leaders clamored to own one.

But times changed quickly for Blackberry. In 2011, this once innovative global company had more than 17,500 employees; in 2014 they were down to 7,000.[5] What happened? How did Blackberry go from dominating the smartphone world to being a relic of the past? Google and Apple happened. Blackberry was blinded by its past success and was out-innovated by Google and Apple. As happened with the typewriter and the VCR, the Blackberry was left behind because the company did not adapt to changes in demand and technology happening around them.

We are no longer in a Black or White America. We are in a multicolored mosaic called America. Therefore, we need gospel-shaped, cross-cultural leaders who act as ambassadors of love, grace, reconciliation, and unity across ethnic, cultural, economic, and generational lines. The fastest-growing, discipleship-oriented, most innovative, community-transforming local churches in the future will be multiethnic, Christ-centered, gospel-shaped churches.

WON'T DIVERSITY JUST HAPPEN?

Just because America is becoming more ethnically diverse doesn't mean that local churches magically will become ethnically diverse along with it. As humans, we tend to be tribal and ethnocentric. We like being with our kind. Our kind is like us, and it's easier to love someone who is like us. This keeps us trapped in bubbles of ignorance.

One survey that focused on 994 people who said they go to church—at least on holidays if not more often—found that:

- 67 percent say their church has done enough to become more ethnically diverse.
- 40 percent want to see more diversity.
- 71 percent of evangelicals say their church is diverse enough.[6]

4

Race and ethnicity reveal sharp differences. Only 37 percent of Whites want their church to be more diverse, compared to 47 percent of Hispanic Americans and 51 percent of African Americans.

Furthermore, in a poll of 1,000 American adults, 82 percent say diversity is good for the country—but not necessarily in their church pews:

- Of the 34 percent of Americans who say they have regularly worshipped in places where they were a minority, one in five of them said their minority status hindered their involvement.
- 22 percent have never experienced being a minority at church, but they think it would make them uncomfortable.
- There's not much urgency about diversity. Half of those surveyed think the churches are "too segregated," but 44 percent disagree.[7]

A survey of 1,000 Protestant senior pastors found 43 percent say they speak about racial reconciliation once a year or less.[8]

One of my great concerns is that we will find ourselves in a multicolored environment throughout the workweek, yet worship in monocolored, monoclass churches on the weekend. Perhaps you're thinking, *What's wrong with that?* That's a fair question. My prayer is that as you read this chapter and the chapters that follow, your heart would be captured by God's dream of filling America and the world with churches that reflect the ethnic diversity, unity, love, and reconciliation that we will find in the new heaven and the new earth. God desires the church of today to be a picture of that great eternal tomorrow. The gospel truth is that God fulfills the Abrahamic covenant through the work of Jesus by the Spirit's power (Galatians 3:8). The new people of God, or the church, is a multiethnic family that displays the wisdom of God (Ephesians 3:6–10). This new multiethnic family is a community of discipleship. Often discipleship in America is about individuals using spiritual disciplines to grow spiritually for personal gain, instead of seeing spiritual growth or discipleship for the health of the body of Christ. The spiritual disciplines themselves are so individualistically oriented, one cannot be surprised they promote individualism. The apostle Paul wrote, "For we were all baptized by one Spirit into one body—whether Jews or Greeks, whether slaves or free—and we were all given one Spirit to drink (1 Corinthians 12:13). It would be quite remarkable for people who were enemies to now become family and friends. This is discipleship. New Testament scholar David DeSilva wrote, "We experience less of God's transforming power where we do not seek this reconciliation across walls of hostility among people of God in Christ (whether racial/national, socioeconomic, and or patriarchal)."[9] When we understand discipleship as communal and cross-cultural, the church is discipled and transformed to stand against racism and injustice.

BLINDED BY SUCCESS AND IMITATION

Often the leaders of homogeneous local churches are blinded by success. A homogeneous church is a church where 80 percent or more of the individuals are of the same ethnicity. Often what we view as ministry success blinds us to God's perspective of successful ministry. Ministry success is an opiate that can take you so high you won't even see the storm of epic change that has *already* arrived. I believe that God, in his providence, has seen fit to raise up leaders who will plant and build multicolored, racial-reconciled local churches that will challenge the status quo and disrupt the norm. I believe these new leaders are measuring successful ministry by a different standard such as racial unity, justice, and discipleship.

WE REPRODUCE WHO WE ARE

As leaders, conference speakers serve as examples and models for others to learn from and emulate. Overwhelmingly, I began to realize I was about the only African American pastor–church planter at the conferences at which I spoke and the only pastor–church planter who had planted a multiethnic, gospel-driven, missional local church. I chose to stop going to conferences as an attendee for several years and only went when invited to speak. I felt as though I was hearing the same stuff from different leaders that produced the same result: homogeneous, middle-class, predominately White churches. In this context, I would share with pastor friends, "Surely my brothers realize America is so much more than the White, suburban, middle-class church? Surely my brothers realize that nonwhite people also live in the suburbs? Surely my brothers realize that performing Asian skits was offensive to our Asian brothers and sisters in the audience who had to endure a White guy poorly acting Asian?

Don't get me wrong. I've learned a lot at conferences, and I'm so appreciative of the support system they offer. I am who I am today because I stand on the shoulders of others. However, thousands and thousands of pastors and church planters in America weekly are learning and imitating others like themselves who lead homogenized churches, whether Black, White, Asian, or Latino. Leaders learning from homogeneous church leaders, therefore, are learning to do ministry and lead churches in a way that perpetuates the homogeneity of the local church. In a multiethnic America, we need a new kind of pastor-leader who desires to be an agent of reconciliation and to build multiethnic local churches because reconciliation is at the heart of the gospel.

RECONCILIATION AT THE HEART OF PAUL'S MINISTRY

When the bride of Christ—his blood-bought, grace-covered, missional ambassadors of reconciliation—remains homogeneous in Christian ghettos, we dishonor King Jesus and the unsearchable riches of his gospel. Sociologist Michael Emerson has found that homogeneous local churches reproduce inequality, encourage oppression, strengthen racial division, and heighten political separation.[10] I also believe that when ethnic diversity is possible and local churches remain homogeneous, the church loses credibility. How can we say Jesus loves everyone when our churches choose to create ministry models that ensure they will remain homogeneous? How can we obey Jesus' instruction that his people become one when we remain segregated? (See John 17:21–23.) Our unity is a witness to the fact that God the Father sent Jesus to rescue the world and that God the Father loves us the way he loved Jesus.

New Testament scholars regard *reconciliation* as the center of Paul's theology and it has been argued that reconciliation is central to the gospel.[11] The church is a reconciled new ethnicity in the Messiah. The cross of Christ brings about peace and reconciliation (Ephesians 2:14–16).

Homogeneous local churches can perpetuate sins like racism. Racism is both individual and structural. When you are only around your tribe or your own kind, you don't have to interact with other ethnicities, so your potential racist attitudes go unchallenged. Homogeneous local churches can perpetuate the sin of classism and inequality. When we choose to be with people of our socioeconomic tribe, we can become callous and dismissive of the plight of others. Homogeneous local churches can perpetuate the sin of systemic injustice. If we know only people like ourselves, our hearts shrink and concerns for others and their struggles never teach us to carry one another's burdens. Homogeneous local churches can perpetuate the sin of economic injustice. We must shift from "Let's help the poor" to "Let's be among the poor and do life with the poor." There is a great opportunity for mutual and beneficial exchanges to take place. When we stay segregated and separated, we find ourselves, as Christians, living in different worlds even though we may be right next door to one another.

On August 9, 2014, Michael Brown, an unarmed eighteen-year-old Black teenager, was shot and killed by a White police officer named Darren Wilson in Ferguson, Missouri, a suburb of Saint

Louis. Before Michael Brown encountered Officer Wilson, he had robbed a convenience store and was walking down the middle of the street. On November 24, 2014, a grand jury decided not to indict the police officer for Brown's death. Riots ensued across America. Black evangelicals and White evangelicals interpreted this situation very differently. For Black Americans, the horror of Black men being lynched came to mind. Anger, fear, and sadness have a context.[12] And for Black Americans that context is the oppression and pain of slavery and injustice that their people have experienced in America for four hundred years. We will continue to interpret events like the Michael Brown shooting very differently as long as we stay segregated in the tribal worlds of Black churches and White churches.

But on May 25, 2020, many of my White brothers and sisters woke up to racial injustice and police brutality. Eight minutes and forty-six seconds—the amount of time a White police officer held his knee on George Floyd's neck, a Black man. Mr. Floyd died a horrific death. Due to COVID-19 putting the world on pause, Americans could not unsee what they saw—they could not look away. Protests erupted not just in America, but around the world.

What if Black and White evangelicals (and Asian and Latino, for that matter) were members of multiethnic churches, living together in community? If this Christ-exalting life were to become our reality, we could address racism, oppression, and injustice in a unified voice of love. What if evangelicals of all ethnicities shared life with one another in a local church community and heard each other's stories and walked in each other's shoes? If this Christ-exalting life were to become our reality, I believe our suspicions and mistrust would be abandoned and replaced with love for one another. The church could actually speak with credibility about the sad events of the Michael Brown shooting and George Floyd's death if we were living examples of ethnic and class reconciliation.

WESTERN INDIVIDUALIST GOSPEL

Our American individualist gospel is obsessed with sending people to heaven when they die, but Jesus and the apostle Paul were more interested in building a church that would bring heaven to earth through redeemed people. Of course we know that to be absent from the body is to be present with the Lord Jesus (see 2 Corinthians 5:8), and I'm grateful for this eternal assurance; however, the gospel is an announcement that there is a King named Jesus who established a kingdom through a multicolored, regenerated people called the church, who are empowered by the Holy Spirit to embody heaven on earth as a foretaste of that which is to come on that great day (see Revelation 5:9–12). This means that as much as we look forward to heaven, there is important, rewarding work to do here on earth. Preeminent New Testament scholar Scot McKnight said this about the local church: "God's desire is for us to experience multiethnic fellowship now in the local church as it will be for eternity. God's heart is total reconciliation."[13]

One of the most beautiful aspects of the gift of salvation is reconciliation, which means enemies have become friends. Through the sinless life, atoning death, resurrection, and ascension of Jesus, God made humanity, which was once his enemy (see Romans 5:8–11), his friend. Thus an ethnically diverse, racist, brutal, unjust, fearful oppressive humanity can be family and friends with one another as a heavenly community on earth.

As I wrote this book, I stood on the shoulders of the leaders who knew that the heart of the gospel is reconciliation. God reconciles humanity to himself and humanity to humanity. I'm thankful to those who have gone before, laboring to see multicolored local churches of love and reconciliation become a reality in America.

I Heard About a Church

In the early 2000s, as God was shaping and molding me, I shared my ideas and dreams of church that would look like heaven and how I could be a living witness to God's grace and human flourishing. Some friends told me about a multiethnic church in Redmond, Washington, pastored by a former NFL player, Ken "Hutch" Hutcherson. Two things in their description immediately grabbed my attention: the possibility of a church that looked like heaven and the fact that it was led by a former NFL player. Several years passed before I actually met Hutch.

In 2008, I was asked to preach at the Antioch Bible Church's men's retreat. This turned out to be a life-defining moment for me. As I stood in the pulpit to proclaim the gospel to these men, I looked into the eyes of multiethnic men, and their communal witness showed me the kind of community the gospel can create. Antioch Bible Church is a heavenly looking community on earth, and it was founded and planted by a reformed racist.

Hutch grew up in Alabama. He hated White people and believed they hated him. He experienced racism and was racist toward White people. The only one who could deal with his racist, hated-filled heart was the one who had a grace-filled, love-filled heart: Jesus. During Hutch's senior year in high school, Jesus tackled him and transformed him. And Jesus took a former racist and planted a church that was 65 percent White and 35 percent Black: Asian, Hispanics, and biracial. Hutch said, "And I married one of the whitest women in the world—a German woman—and we have four beautiful chocolate German children!"[14]

At the men's retreat, Hutch and some of the elders prayed over me. They commissioned me to be a multiethnic church planter. I don't think I understood the significance then, but I do now. Hutch has gone on to be with Jesus now, but the impression he left on my life is as strong today as it was when I worshiped that weekend at Antioch Bible Church. As I sat next to Hutch and his wife, my heart was exploding. At Antioch Bible Church, I knew a multiethnic church forged by grace and the blood of Jesus could be planted. I saw it. I experienced it. Thank you, Hutch; you were a mentor and a friend.

Australian New Testament scholar Michael F. Bird wrote: "The gospel is lived out when Christians practice reconciliation among themselves and exemplify it before their neighbors. The Ambassadors for reconciliation have the opportunity to promote peacemaking in communities rife with factions, distrust, and mutual suspicions."[15] Isn't that beautiful? Our world needs more beauty like this coming from our local churches.

Right now, the church in America does not exemplify reconciliation, which is the heartbeat of the gospel and God's longing for humanity. The average church in America is ethnically and socio-economically segregated; granted, sometimes this is because of demographics, but most of the time it's by choice fueled by *indifference, prejudices, petty preferences,* or *ignorance of the gospel.* Instead of being fueled by Jesus' heart for reconciliation, we are fueled by the status quo.

Preeminent New Testament scholar N. T. Wright said that the apostle Paul's "aims and intentions can be summarized under the word *katallage,* 'reconciliation.'"[16] Paul, the original gospel-shaped leader and champion of multiethnic, Christocentric, missional church planting, wrote these Holy Spirit–inspired words in an ethnically and socioeconomically segregated Greco-Roman world:

> All this is from God, who through Christ reconciled us to himself and gave us the ministry of reconciliation; that is, in Christ God was reconciling the world to himself, not counting their trespasses against them, and entrusting to us the message of reconciliation. Therefore, we are ambassadors for Christ, God making his appeal through us. We implore you on behalf of Christ, be reconciled to God. (2 Corinthians 5:18–20)

Pastor, church planter, elder, and Christ-follower, you have been entrusted with the ministry of reconciliation! This calling is not optional. This calling is not debatable. The only question is, Will you be obedient and accept this divine invitation to walk in your calling as a reconciler? Will you learn how to be a gospel-shaped leader who leads the church into our multicolored world?

Please listen to the apostle Paul's heart. Hear him cry out, "All this is from God, who through Christ reconciled us to himself and gave us the ministry of reconciliation" (2 Corinthians 5:18). God, through Paul, has implored us to be ministers of reconciliation just as he implored the Jews and Gentiles in Corinth to be reconciled as one body in local churches! Our vertical reconciliation to God infuses us with the indwelling life of Jesus and the sealing presence of God the Holy Spirit, which empowers us to live in horizontal relationships in the local church with ethnically and socioeconomically different people for the glory of God.

The apostle Paul envisioned and built local churches of reconciliation where ethnocentrism, classism, and sexism were crucified on the bloody cross of Christ and by his resurrection power. "There is neither Jew nor Greek [ethnocentrism], there is neither slave nor free [classism], there is no male and female [sexism], for you are all one in Christ Jesus" (Galatians 3:28). Do you feel the weight of this gospel reality?

THE BOOK OF ROMANS

Even the glorious book of Romans is not about our Western arguments about Calvinism, Amyraldism, and Arminianism. The book of Romans is about how the gospel empowers Jews and Gentiles to express God's glory by living in harmony as a diverse community of reconciliation on earth as God's fulfillment of the covenant promise made to Abraham in direct opposition to the brutal first-century Greco-Roman world:

> May the God of endurance and encouragement grant you to live
> in such harmony with one another [Jews and Gentiles], in accord
> with Christ Jesus, that together you may with one voice glorify

the God and Father of our Lord Jesus Christ. Therefore welcome one another as Christ has welcomed you, for the glory of God.

For I tell you that Christ became a servant to the circumcised to show God's truthfulness, in order to confirm the promises given to the patriarchs, and in order that the Gentiles might glorify God for his mercy. As it is written,

> "Therefore I will praise you among the Gentiles,
> and sing to your name."
> And again it is said,
> "Rejoice, O Gentiles, with his people."

And again,

> "Praise the Lord, all you Gentiles,
> and let all the peoples extol him."
> And again Isaiah says,
> "The root of Jesse will come,
> even he who arises to rule the Gentiles;
> in him will the Gentiles hope."

May the God of hope fill you with all joy and peace in believing, so that by the power of the Holy Spirit you may abound in hope. (Romans 15:5–13)

Pastors, church planters, and Christ-followers, if you care about the future of the church in America, you must care about learning how to partner with the Holy Spirit in creating multicolored,

Jesus-exalting, missional congregations that can reach a changing America and give a foretaste of Jesus' eternal kingdom. If the church in America is not just to survive but to thrive, it must be multiethnic in the twenty-first century.[17]

REACHING BACK INTO THE PAST

One of the gospel innovations that caused the early church to flourish and experience rapid growth in the first-century world was that the Jesus movement "overwhelmed ethnic barriers" and God birthed a new multicolored ethnicity, called the church.[18] Paul was shaped by a deep belief that God made a promise to Abraham (Galatians 3:8; Ephesians 2:12). At the heart of this promise was that God would give Abraham a multiethnic, reconciled family that acted as God's agents of grace in the world. He boldly proclaimed God's heart for reconciliation in the face of violent opposition:

> For he himself is our peace, who has made us both one and has broken down in his flesh the dividing wall of hostility by abolishing the law of commandments expressed in ordinances, that he might create in himself one new man in place of the two, so making peace, and might *reconcile* us both to God in one body through the cross, thereby killing the hostility. (Ephesians 2:14–16, emphasis added)

The local churches of 2050 will be the churches of today that reach back to the first century and rediscover the Christ-exalting, gospel-shaped, missional innovation of the early church led by Paul that produced multiethnic local churches. The churches of that time were made up of Jews and Gentiles (Africans, Asians, Greeks, Romans, barbarians, etc.) as well as rich and poor. This diversity shocked and rocked the harsh, segregated Greco-Roman world. These early diverse congregations displayed a better way to live, love, and be human. The early church was a picture of what was to come for Jesus' blood-bought, Spirit-sealed people:

> And they sang a new song, saying,
> "Worthy are you to take the scroll
> and to open its seals,
> for you were slain, and by your blood you ransomed
>   people for God from every tribe and language and
>   people and nation,
> and you have made them a kingdom and priests to our
>   God, and they shall reign on the earth."

Then I looked, and I heard around the throne and the living creatures and the elders the voice of many angels, numbering myriads of myriads and thousands of thousands, saying with a loud voice,

> "Worthy is the Lamb who was slain,
> to receive power and wealth and wisdom and might
> and honor and glory and blessing!" (Revelation 5:9–12)

We can do the same. We must do the same.

TWO STEPS FORWARD, ONE STEP BACK

Just as the sun rises over the horizon, multiethnic churches are rising in America. In 1998, only 6 percent of all US congregations were multiethnic; that rose to 8 percent in 2007, 12 percent in 2012, and 16 percent in 2019. This means that no one ethnic group had more than 80 percent of the people in the congregation.[19] Only 7 percent of evangelical churches were multiethnic in 1998, however, in 2019, that skyrocketed to 22 percent[20] and 58 percent of megachurches are multiethnic.[21] This is up from 36 percent in 2000. According to Michael Emerson, diverse megachurches are

1. better at incorporating new people into the life of the congregation,
2. have more immigrants, and
3. have more new people come in the past five years than non-diverse megachurches.[22]

On the surface the increase in multiethnic congregations looks good. And some of it is good. However, as we get underneath the numbers, multiethnic megachurches are more likely the result of the perceived upward mobility of the megachurch, pragmatic, user-friendly sermons, fun kids programming, or even the musical style. It is not the result of a theological conviction and the inclusion of minority leadership. Emerson, Dougherty, and Chaves wrote,

"For whites, diversity is pursued by trying to attract people of color who will not challenge white congregants' views and practices, sometimes even assuring this selectivity by interacting with potential black participants in ways that ensure that those unwilling to accommodate white culture will not return."[23]

Sadly, many multiethnic megachurches are silent on issues of racial justice and systemic injustice.[24] Recently, many minorities have left these kinds of churches because it was a "thin" diversity that lacked commitment to a holistic, gospel-shaped diversity, in which accommodation is realized, not simply assimilation. In 2018, the *Detroit Times* published, "Why Are People of Color Leaving White Evangelical Churches?"

> The exodus started the day after the George Zimmerman verdict. We were mourning. And we went to church on Sunday morning hoping we would hear a word of comfort. And many of us who went to either multi-racial or predominately white spaces found no word of comfort. We found no word at all.[25]

Of note, the White church expects and sees it as normative that Asians, Latinos and African Americans will come to their church and make it diverse. But the idea of White brothers and sisters going to minority-led churches where they would be the minority is not considered a serious option.[26]

In 2018–2019, about 7 out 10 multiethnic churches were led by White men, 2 in 10 had a Black led pastor, and 1 in 10 had a Latino or Asian led pastor.[27] In the White churches, half of the congregation were nonwhite, but the pastoral staff overwhelming was majority

White. People of color on those staffs had very little to no author-ity.[28] Their color was more like a *decoration* instead of a *declaration* of the gospel (Ephesians 3:5–11).

One of the drawbacks of being a majority-culture person is a lack of awareness to one's cultural blind spots. How do you tell a fish that it is in water? Water is all it knows. The fish must experi-ence life outside of the water to realize that water is not normative to non-fish. The gospel-shaped reality of ethnic and culturally diverse leadership helps us to see our blind spots and helps us to see that one cultural expression is not normative to all people. It is our differences that make us better. Jesus reflects his glory in and through multiethnic family in beautiful ways. This beauty makes us beautiful.

WHAT WE NEED

We need multiethnic churches with ethnically diverse leader-ship, as in the early church in Antioch (see Acts 6:1–7). We need multiethnic churches that address all sin issues, including racism, injustice, and oppression from a gospel-inspired perspective like the early church (see Acts 6:1–7; Galatians 3:24–28; Colossians 3:11; Romans 15:6–7).

We need multiethnic churches in urban, suburban, and rural areas. We need multiethnic churches that show the world what rec-onciliation looks like (see Colossians 3:10). We need multiethnic local churches that give America hope that humanity can live in love and harmony (see Romans 15:5–12). We need leaders who are saturated in a gospel vision of unity in divided culture.

STUDY QUESTIONS, REFLECTIONS, AND PRAYER

1. As you read the statistics in chapter 1 about the changing face of America, what thoughts and emotions did you experience? How does your city, neighborhood, school, or workplace reflect this changing demographic?

2. In light of how diverse America is becoming, on a scale of 1 to 10 (with 1 being the worst and 10 being the best), how prepared is your church to reach the diversity in your ministry context? On a scale of 1 to 10 (with 1 being not important at all and 10 being very important), how important do you think ethnic diversity in your church is to your congregation? What about socioeconomic diversity?

3. "Sociologist Michael Emerson has found that homogeneous local churches reproduce inequality, encourage oppression, strengthen racial division, and heighten political separation." Why do you think this would be true? What do you think the role of the church is in changing these facts?

4. Read Ephesians 2:14–16. Think about its implications in your community and church. What is one thing your church could do to encourage reconciliation among people?

5. Read Revelation 5:9–12. With that passage in mind, what does this statement imply: "A leader captivated by a gospel vision for unity in diversity is a leader who is so passionate about the glory of God being revealed through the local church that he or she is willing to learn how to be a cross-cultural, gospel-of-grace preaching, organizational-strategizing,

leader-developing disciple of people who partners with the Lord Jesus in building local churches that reflect the future of the church in the present."

PRAYER

Father, may your passion to bring heaven to earth through the finished work of Jesus by the Spirit's power inspire us to have a new vision for the church, a vision that reflects Revelation 5:9–12: a gospel vision of love, grace, and reconciliation. Father, give us faith, courage, and, above all, love so we can fulfill this sacred task. We pray this in Jesus' name. Amen.

TWO

Seeing Life for the First Time

I once was lost but now am found.
Was blind, but now I see.
—John Newton, "Amazing Grace"

GOD USES THE UNLIKELY

As a little boy, I never wanted to be a pastor because I had no clue what a pastor was. As you read my story, you will be just as shocked as I am that I am pastor writing a book on how to build multiethnic churches. But God loves to use the unlikely, doesn't he? Here is my story of becoming a follower of Jesus and a pastor with a gospel vision to see racially reconciled multiethnic churches.

My story begins on April 9, 1971, when my seventeen-year-old mother gave birth to me at Robert B. Green Hospital in downtown San Antonio, Texas. My nineteen-year-old father looked on with my grandparents and uncle as I entered the world. We don't choose our family, and we don't choose the story; we are born into our family's story. And we don't choose the blessings or curses that follow from those facts.

The reality is that we are all born into Adam's family of darkness and death, and that's why we all need to be *reborn* into Jesus' family of light and life.

MY FAMILY

My mom went to high school in the tumultuous late 1960s and early 1970s when America was being desegregated. She was bussed out of poverty on the west side of San Antonio to a predominately White, middle-class high school. To give you some context, the first time my mom and her twin brother saw White people was in 1963, when they were nine years old! My uncle asked my grandmother, "Who are these blue people?"

In high school, my mom played the violin but was told by a White music teacher, "There's really no need for you to learn the violin anymore, because people like you become maids." My mom told me that this crushed her fragile heart. And when you add this humiliation to her past traumas, it's no wonder she labeled herself as damaged goods.

When she was pregnant with me during her junior year in high school, the school nurse told her to abort me. But my mom said, "No, I'm not killing my baby!" And as I write these words, my heart is seized with gratefulness. I've lived an amazing life that almost did not happen had my momma not displayed the courage to give me a chance at life.

My parents never got married, so by the time I was six, my father was out of my life. He and my mom could never have peace with each other, probably because their bruised hearts were not at peace. My dad saw me play flag football when I was in fifth grade, which was the last time he ever saw me play football. Until God the Father fathered me, I was angry and bitter over my dad missing out on being in my life. The Father's love empowered me to love and restore my relationship with my dad.

My grandparents primarily raised me. Granny was my best friend. During college and even during my NFL years, I would call her just about every day to talk. I loved that woman. She always believed in me and always encouraged me.

When I was a young teen, she said, "Dewey, you are not like the rest of us." I didn't know what that meant at the time, and to some degree, I still don't. What I do know is that, until recently, I was the only male in my family over the age of twenty to graduate from high school or college. I was the only one not to have a drug or alcohol addiction, not to spend time in jail, and not to have a child outside of marriage.

My grandfather provided me with food and shelter. But not just me. He took care of and provided for a lot of people in my family. His greatest gift to me was his work ethic. Every day he went to his little convenience store, where he was owner, accountant, human resources director, manager, and janitor. When I was about seventeen, our relationship transformed drastically for the better. During my senior year of high school, I was named KENS-TV San Antonio

High School Player of the Week and was interviewed by the sports anchor, Dan Cook. The interview played on a Sunday morning as my grandpa was getting ready for work. When he saw my face and heard my voice on television, his eyes lit up. It was as if I were a totally different person to him. I now know that the light in his eyes was hope—hope that I would make something of my life.

GROWING UP

I grew up in the midst of criminal activity, violence, poverty, and epic dysfunction. Our house was a tiny, dilapidated, roach-infested thing, but it was our home. Our family had a quasi–Jehovah's Witness background.

We never prayed together. We never ate dinner together. We never went to the Kingdom Hall, which is the Jehovah's Witness version of church. To me, Jehovah was a good luck charm that I would ask for favors from time to time.

Because I had a cousin who was four years older than I was, I hung out around older guys in the neighborhood. In my hood, there were Mexicans and Black people. However, one White dude did hang out with us. We called him Golden Boy because he had long blond hair that would blow in the wind as he rode his bike.

I'm indebted to the older boys I grew up with because they taught me how to play football. Those formative years of playing football on the streets of San Antonio's west side created a passion in me that fueled my future.

I was not a very good middle school football player. I was small and slow. I was an average football player as a freshman and sophomore at Fox Tech High School. But then my family moved, and I transferred to Converse Judson High School, where I was coached by D. W. Rutledge.

Judson is one of the elite high school football programs in America. Coach Rutledge is a Texas high school football legend, and he has been inducted into numerous halls of fame. My first year at Judson was hard mentally and physically, because I couldn't keep up with the other players' tempo, intensity, and execution. But Coach Rutledge and Coach Mike Sullivan, Judson's defensive back coach, saw something in me that I didn't see in myself. They pushed me further than I thought I could go. They forged mental toughness in me. They taught me that adversity is an opportunity. These men stepped in for the father I never had.

So much of what I learned about leadership was taught to me on the Judson practice fields. The Judson football team was a collection of multiethnic, socioeconomically diverse, D. W. Rutledge followers. He was our pastor, the assistant coaches were his staff, and we, the players, were the congregation.

We had White boys who rocked cowboy boots with big belt buckles and listened to George Strait; Black dudes who rocked high-top fades, wore Air Jordans, and listened to Run–D.M.C.; and Asian and Latino guys who did their own thing. We had rich kids, middle-class kids, and welfare kids. At Judson, I learned the beauty and power of diversity.

My high school football team was better because we were a diverse team. Embracing our different experiences made us better together. Our common vision was the glue that bonded us together so we could play as one team.

THE POWER OF DIVERSITY

As players, we'd run through a brick wall for Coach Rutledge. (I'd be willing to do it to this day, but if I tried, I'd pull my hamstring or my bum left knee would collapse before I got to it.) Why would my teammates and I do this? Because we knew Coach Rutledge loved us. A true leader loves the people he or she leads, not because of what they can produce, but because they have intrinsic worth as human beings.

After my football career was complete at Judson in 1989, Coach Sullivan took me to his office, put a floppy disk into a computer, and helped me study for the ACT. The minimum score I could get on the ACT to receive a football scholarship was 16. After taking the test three times, my scores were combined, and I reached 16. This would not have happened if Coach Sullivan had not loved me enough to help me succeed off the field in the game of life. Because of Coach Rutledge and Coach Sullivan and my teammates, I was voted to the All-Time San Antonio Texas High School Football Team.

FINDING A GOD TO WORSHIP

By the end of my senior year at Judson, football became so much more than just a game to me. I recognized that football gave me a new life and potentially could give me the kind of life I had seen on television. This life would be one of happiness, money, sweet cars, and girls. I believed this would allow me to save my family from the demons that had up to now terrorized them by giving them money.

Football was more than a game; it was salvation. It was my ticket out of the hell I was in. I had to make it in football. If I didn't, I had nothing. In football, I found what my heart ached for: a god to worship. Everyone, even an atheist, worships something or someone. I define worship as finding something or someone from which you derive a sense of love, a perceived identity, and a mission that drives you toward a goal. It might be education or philosophical naturalism. It may be fame, money, power, or sex. But we were all created for worship.

In football, if I played well, I received love. In football, I had an identity that gave me significance—I was a great football player. I was somebody. In football, I had a mission—I was going to college and then hopefully to the NFL. This would allow me to rescue my family and to live the American Dream.

BYU: The Mormon University

At the end of my senior football season, I found myself choosing between scholarship offers from Texas Christian University (TCU) and Brigham Young University (BYU). I chose BYU for three reasons: (1) I could play for legendary coach Lavell Edwards; (2) my family could see me play, because BYU games were always carried on ESPN; and (3) it is in Provo, Utah, which was far from Texas. I hate to write that, but I really wanted to escape the dysfunction of my family environment.

So I left Judson, a multiethnic, socioeconomically diverse community and moved to Utah, an overwhelmingly White, Mormon community. I experienced a true culture shock! During my first week, I kept wondering, *What planet am I on?* As I look back at the sovereign hand of God, I see how my four years at BYU helped me in planting and leading a multiethnic church. My BYU experience taught me how to integrate, and I learned how to get along with people vastly different from me.

I had some wonderful experiences at BYU. I met my wife, Vicki, there. Growing up, I never had visions of getting married, because no one in my immediate family ever got married. In fact, the first wedding I ever attended was my own. Vicki changed all of that for me, and we have been married for twenty-three years. I love her. She's my best friend and greatest encourager, outside of Jesus.

I was voted to the BYU Football All-Time Dream Team, meaning I was considered one of the greatest players in the history of BYU football.[1] After four years of worshiping my god (football) there, I was ready to go to the heaven called the National Football League. And that's when my god began to let me down.

DRAFT DAY

On April 25, 1993, my wife and I, along with my brother and sister-in-law, were in my tiny four-hundred-square-foot apartment watching the NFL draft. During the draft, my mom kept calling me. Back in those days, we didn't have call-waiting, so, eventually, I had to tell my mom, "Stop calling me! If the NFL does call, I won't be able to talk to them because you keep calling!"

The first day of the draft was about to end when the phone rang again. I thought it was my mom again, so I picked it up and said, "Hello," in an impatient, slightly annoyed voice. Then I heard, "This is Clyde Powers of the Indianapolis Colts. We have selected you as the ninety-second pick in the 1993 NFL draft." My wife started crying because she saw my name on ESPN: "Colts select defensive back Derwin Gray out of Brigham Young University."

We went bananas! We rushed to the mall and bought an Indianapolis Colts hat. I thought, *I did it! I made it. Life will be awesome!* I had an expectation of what was to come, but things were about to change.

THE NAKED PREACHER

When the Colts drafted me, I quickly realized there was a guy on the team who was different. Every day after practice, one of my teammates, a six-foot-two, 240-pound linebacker, would take a shower, dry off, and wrap a towel around his waist. He would then engage my teammates in conversations about Jesus. He would ask, "Do you know Jesus?" Because I didn't grow up in church, I had no clue what he was talking about. The only thing running through my mind was, *Do you know you're half-naked?*

Out of curiosity, I asked some of the veterans, "What's up with the half-naked Black man walking around talking about 'Do you know Jesus?'" And they said, "Don't pay any attention to him. That's the Naked Preacher." His real name was Steve Grant. So every day after practice the Naked Preacher lived as a missionary, sharing the love of Jesus with his teammates.

One day he asked me, "Rookie, D. Gray, do you know Jesus?" That question started a five-year-long conversation with the Naked Preacher.

After three years with the Colts, I found myself somewhat wealthy, a team captain, a celebrity, the husband of a beautiful woman, and a father. I was able to send money home to Texas to "fix" my family. Everything was supposed to be okay, right? I achieved the American Dream, but my life was a living nightmare. Outwardly, I had everything, but my possessions and accomplishments could not heal the interior of my life. Money didn't fix me. Fame didn't fix me. My wife couldn't fix me. Having a daughter didn't fix me. And sending money to my family didn't fix them.

I knew, for the players, NFL stood for "not for long." If football gave me an identity and a mission, who would I be after that identity and mission went away? This really scared me. I lived in fear—fear of knowing that one day I wouldn't be an NFL player.

And to make matters worse, after my third season in the NFL, my body started to break down. At the beginning of my fourth season, I was injured a lot. I started to think, *God is trying to tell me something.*

In 1997 at Anderson College, where the Colts held training camp every summer, I walked to my dorm room after lunch one day. As I walked, something was happening in my heart that words couldn't explain. I now know it was God's Holy Spirit ministering grace to me so I could see my need for Jesus.

When I got to the dorm, I picked up the phone and called Vicki. I said, "Sweetheart, I want to be committed to you, and I want to be committed to Jesus." My wife had become a follower of Jesus through the witnessing of women at her job a few months earlier, and we remain thankful for the Christ-followers who saw themselves as missionaries in the workplace.

SEEING LIFE FOR THE FIRST TIME

After I got off the phone, I felt God's unfailing, soul-satisfying love for the first time. I sat in that dorm room and cried and cried.

I didn't know God's love could be so beautiful. For the first time I could see the cross and what Jesus did for me. For the first time I could see that I was loved, not because of my performance, but I was loved *in spite of* my performance. I was forgiven, not because I deserved it, but because Jesus gave me a blood bath. I was graced, not because I earned it, but because Jesus lavished it on me as a gift.

On August 2, 1997, I fell in love with Jesus because he loved me with a love that is unsurpassed and unequaled. In Jesus, I found the unconditional love, the identity, and the mission I had looked for my entire life. Soon after meeting Jesus in a dark dorm room, I began to see life differently.

CAROLINA PANTHERS

From 1993 to 1997, I played for the Indianapolis Colts, and then God moved us to Charlotte, North Carolina, to play football for the Carolina Panthers. I figured I would play another five years and have a ten-year NFL career, but my plan didn't quite work out. While playing against the Dallas Cowboys, I ran downfield on kickoff coverage as I had a thousand other times. I engaged a blocker. He turned me to my left, but my left knee turned right. In that moment, I heard and felt the bone break and some knee ligaments snap like rubber bands. And then my professional football career was over.

As a result of my left knee injury, I was placed on injured reserve by the Panthers, which meant I still received my full salary but didn't play in any games. I spent the entire 1998 season rehabilitating my knee and reading the Bible. In essence, God in his sovereignty arranged my life so I could study the Bible for hours a day and get paid five hundred thousand dollars to do it. In the midst of my disappointment, God was preparing me for his appointment to plant Transformation Church.

Three significant things happened as a result of my knee injury:

1. My injury weaned my dependence on football and strengthened my dependence on Jesus.
2. I studied the Bible each day, and my mind was transformed. I had a playbook as a football player, and God had a playbook called the Bible. Knowing my playbook well meant I played better on the field, so I reasoned that if I knew God's playbook, I could play better in the game of life.
3. I would use my income—two hundred thousand dollars after taxes and agent fees—to start a ministry in 1999.

GOD, WHY ME?

In the summer of 1999, Vicki and I both sensed it was time to close the book on my NFL career, although we had no clue as to what we were going to do next. Around that time, I received a phone call from a youth pastor with the South Carolina Baptist Association. He asked me to share my testimony with a couple thousand students prior to a University of South Carolina football game. I told him I needed to pray about it, because I wasn't sure God had picked the right person to speak at this event. I was thinking, *God, really! Of all the people you could choose to tell these students about your grace, you choose me—a stutterer.*

I remember wrestling with God in the shower as tears flooded down my face. I kept saying to him, *I can't do this. I'm a stutterer. God, people laugh at me when I attempt to talk.* In the midst of my saying what I couldn't do, I sensed two truths that have anchored themselves in my heart:

1. If Jesus, the Eternal Son of God, can die for my sins and rise to new life, the Holy Spirit can give me the ability to preach the unsearchable riches of Christ.
2. If Jesus' grace has utterly transformed my life, who am I to resist sharing his epic story of grace? My testimony was his testimony of grace. I was a trophy of grace, and I had been *commissioned* to share it.

I went to Columbia with Vicki and our baby daughter. I shared Jesus' story of grace in my life with note cards falling out of my pockets, and I cried a lot while I talked. For twenty-six years of my life I was taught not to cry because it was a sign of weakness. Actually my lack of crying was the result of a hard, wounded heart. But when grace broke into my heart, a dam broke and tears of joy flowed.

At the end of my first sermon, I said, "Do you all want what happened to me to happen to you?"

Eventually the youth pastor who invited me to preach walked onto the platform and gave a real invitation and hundreds of kids stood up to receive Jesus.

Afterward the youth pastor said to me, "Get ready! God's going start using you." I had no clue what that meant. But I would find out the next day.

The next day my phone started ringing with invitations to share my testimony at churches, men's events, and conferences. Vicki booked and organized my travel, and I went to share my testimony of grace.

After traveling the country and preaching the gospel for several years, I was deeply bothered and confused by something I saw everywhere I preached. I was disturbed by the fact that the nightclubs I used to party in, the football teams I played on (other than BYU), the high school I attended, and the military in America were all ethnically diverse, but the churches and conferences I preached at were segregated gatherings. During the week I lived in an ethnically integrated world, and on weekends, in the American Christian world, I traveled back in time to a segregated America. As a young Christian who had grown up with no church background, I thought the church was supposed to be the one community that would bring people together, not divide them. Everywhere I traveled and preached, I saw how pastors developed methodologies of doing church that actually divided people based on ethnicity, cultural preferences, and socioeconomic status.

I Asked the Wrong Question

I began to ask pastors and seminary professors why the church was the most ethnically segregated institution in America. The answers I received were ridiculous, unbiblical, racist, and cowardly.

A Black pastor said, "I don't like White people! You can't trust them! The only time we can be Black in a White-dominated culture is in church on Sunday. This is our time. Plus, White people will never submit to the leadership of a Black man."

A White suburban megachurch pastor explained, "If my church became diverse, many of the White fathers would be afraid that their daughters would date and marry Black men. I can't risk that happening."

A Latino pastor warned me that if I planted a multiethnic church, I would "steal his people." I thought all people belong to Jesus.

An Asian pastor told me, "Our culture and language are more important than reaching the non-Asians in our community."

As a young follower of Jesus, I was dazed and confused by the nonsense I was hearing.

If the apostle Paul were alive today, I think he would be greatly disappointed. He would rebuke the American church for its seg-regation and lack of gospel understanding. It is an irrefutable fact that Paul and Barnabas planted multiethnic churches. They didn't plant a church for Jews, another for Greeks, another for Arabs, and another for Syrians. Biblical scholar Christopher J. H. Wright wrote in *The Mission of God* that Paul and Barnabas were "the first to establish whole communities of believers, from mixed Jewish and Gentile backgrounds—that is, to plant multiethnic churches."[2] So you want to be like the apostle Paul? Begin by forming real, multi-ethnic relationships, then focus on building multiethnic local churches like he did.

By 2004 I became angry by what I saw as an offense to King Jesus and his beautiful community-forming gospel. I sensed God saying to me, "Derwin, don't criticize. Create." I hadn't wanted to be a pastor because my life experience taught me that if people got close to me, they would hurt me. However, God had other plans that he needed to awaken inside of me.

As a football player, I was a student of the game. When I became a follower of Jesus, I became a student of the Bible. As a result of this passion to learn, I went to seminary. While taking a New Testament course at Southern Evangelical Seminary, I could see Ephesians 4:7–16 clearly:

But grace was given to each one of us according to the measure of Christ's gift. Therefore it says, "When he ascended on high he led a host of captives, and he gave gifts to men."

(In saying, "He ascended," what does it mean but that he had also descended into the lower regions, the earth? He who descended is the one who also ascended far above all the heavens, that he might fill all things.) And he gave the apostles, the prophets, the evangelists, the shepherds and teachers, to equip the saints for the work of ministry, for building up the body of Christ, until we all attain to the unity of the faith and of the knowledge of the Son of God, to mature manhood, to the measure of the stature of the fullness of Christ, so that we may no longer be children, tossed to and fro by the waves and carried about by every wind of doctrine, by human cunning, by craftiness in deceitful schemes. Rather, speaking the truth in love, we are to grow up in every way into him who is the head, into Christ, from whom the whole body, joined and held together by every joint with which it is equipped, when each part is working properly, makes the body grow so that it builds itself up in love.

To me, the words of this text jumped off the page. Sitting in that classroom I knew God had called and gifted me to lead a multiethnic church. So I made a deal with God. I said, "God, if I do this, it can't be a segregated church! There are enough of those! It has to be a church where Asian people, Latino people, White people, Black people, and ethnically mixed people would come together and be one in Christ. If I do this, Father, it has be a diverse church like the church in the new heaven and the new earth."

Over the next few years I attended a local church—a suburban, homogeneous megachurch—while God shaped me through my years in seminary and continued ministry as an itinerant evangelist. I attended a conference at Willow Creek and deeply sensed God's speaking to my heart that I would be a pastor, not just a speaker, very soon.

I called Vicki and said, "Sweetie, I think God is calling me to pastor." All I heard was silence. My wife had been as opposed to pastoring as much as I was. Then I said, "If God is calling me to pastor, he will affirm this call in your heart too."

Church Planting 101

Over the next few months, God confirmed our call to pastor a church. I use the words "our call" because everything my wife and I do, we do as a team. Vicki is anointed with the gift of administration. She was valedictorian in high school and college, so she's really smart and is a great strategist and organizational leader. So, basically, I married Superwoman.

Eventually, God led me to partner with some local pastors to launch a church where I learned a lot about what to do and what not to do as a church planter. For example, three lead pastors is an awesome idea on paper, but in reality, not so much. So, with a lot of passion, a lot of inexperience, and a lot of emotional immaturity, we launched a church in January 2007.

God continued to grow my desire to plant a gospel-centered, multiethnic local church. Eventually the day came when the lead pastors went off on their own, choosing to multiply rather than divide God's church. In the spring of 2009, Vicki, our best friend, Angela, and I began preparing to plant Transformation Church. Our congregation prayed and decided which new church plant they'd join. One group of people went with my copastor, and 178 others felt called to partner with me. We overcame the initial challenges of finding a place to hold services—we ended up in a warehouse in Indian Land, South Carolina, which is close to Charlotte, North Carolina. It was a tough process, launching a church with dust and chewing gum in our pockets, but God did it anyway.

On February 7, 2010—Super Bowl Sunday—we had our first worship services. I came up with the crazy idea to launch with two services even though I didn't think anyone was going to show up, not even the 178 people who made up our church planting team. And even if they did show up, we would still have a lot of empty seats in both services. Despite my fears, I prayed for 700 people to come. Looking back, I would have never prayed such a faith-filled, courageous prayer if I had any clue that 700 people was a lot to expect for a church plant's first services.

At the end of the second service that beautiful day, executive pastor Paul Allen looked me in the eye, with tears flowing down his face, and said, "Pastor, 701 showed up." Then I started crying. As a new church, God shattered all the growth barriers in one weekend. Ever since that opening Sunday, God has grown Transformation

Church like crazy. I feel like we are experiencing what happened in the book of Acts: "And the Lord added to their number day by day those who were being saved" (2:47).

I was told by pastors and church planters, "Don't plant a multi-ethnic church. It's hard. Those churches don't grow. The offering is terrible. People in America want to be with their own people."

In our first year as a local church, we were the second-fastest-growing church in America by percentage, and then in 2011, 2012, and 2013, we remained one of the one hundred fastest-growing churches in America.[3]

I believe Jesus is longing for pastors to ask him to do a work that can be explained only by his power. Trust Jesus to move some mountains so he can be glorious and beautiful in the world through his bride, the church.

Salvation is inseparable from being in Jesus' church. But what is salvation? Let's take a look in chapter 3.

STUDY QUESTIONS, REFLECTIONS, AND PRAYER

1. What's your story? How did you become a follower of Jesus?
2. "Gospel-shaped leaders learn how to integrate and how to get along with people who are vastly different from them." Name three ways you have experienced this in your life. If you can't, consider three ways you could increase your relationships with people who are of a different ethnicity than you.
3. So you want to be like the apostle Paul? Begin by forming real,

multiethnic relationships, then focus on building multiethnic local churches like he did. Do you find this intimidating? What are some ways you can increase your relationships with people in other ethnic or socioeconomic groups?

4. Who are the people you are in deep relationship with that are of a different ethnicity and class than you? What is something you have learned from them?

5. After reading my story, what are some aspects of your story that God may be using to prepare you to build or lead a multiethnic, multiclass church?

PRAYER

Father, bless me to live a multiethnic life. Bring people into my life who are of a different ethnicity and class so I can have the honor of sharing life with them. Bless me to sit at their feet, hear their stories, learn about their struggles, and celebrate their victories. I pray this in Jesus' name and in the Spirit's power, amen.

THREE

SEEING SALVATION THROUGH THE LENS OF UPWARD, INWARD, OUTWARD

But the Lord said to me, "Go, for I will send you far away to the Gentiles!" The crowd listened until Paul said that word. Then they all began to shout, "Away with such a fellow! He isn't fit to live!" They yelled, threw off their coats, and tossed handfuls of dust into the air.

—ACTS 22:21–23 NLT

THE VISION: UPWARD, INWARD, OUTWARD

A vision of the future transforms what you do today. If you hang around Transformation Church for very long, you will hear this

Derwinism over and over. Transformation Church was built on Jesus' vision for humanity. If you are going to be gospel-formed leaders and lead a multiethnic, socioeconomically diverse local church, you must grow in your ability to cast a vision. I define *vision casting* as the God-inspired ability to see a future that does not yet exist but should. This future is so Christ-exalting and life-giving that people run into the future and drag it back to the present.

Before Transformation Church ever existed, she existed in my heart. I could picture a congregation of White people, Asian people, Black people, Latino people, and every other kind of people: young, old, poor, middle class, and rich. My wife and I, along with our friend Angela, turned our dining room into the Transformation Church Strategy Room in the summer of 2009. For weeks we crafted the vision statement. We knew we needed our vision rooted in Jesus' heart so it would be the fuel that moved Transformation Church toward fulfilling its purpose.

You can't cast an authentic vision if you aren't embodying it. Jesus won my heart with his vision; it transformed my life. And I wanted it to transform others' lives.

Jesus' vision for humanity was the Great Commandment:

And he said to him, "You shall love the Lord your God with all your heart and with all your soul and with all your mind. This is the great and first commandment. And the second is like it: You shall love your neighbor as yourself. On these two commandments depend all the Law and the Prophets." (Matthew 22:37–40)

And the Great Commission:

And Jesus came and said to them, "All authority in heaven and on earth has been given to me. Go therefore and make disciples of all nations, baptizing them in the name of the Father and of the Son and of the Holy Spirit, teaching them to observe all that I have commanded you. And behold, I am with you always, to the end of the age." (Matthew 28:18–20)

We decided that Transformation Church would be a Great Commandment–Great Commission local church empowered by the great grace and life of our Lord Jesus. We say our vision like this: *Transformation Church is a multiethnic, multigenerational, mission-shaped community that loves God completely (Upward), ourselves correctly (Inward), and our neighbors compassionately (Outward).*[1] To make our vision memorable we say, "Upward, Inward, Outward" because what's memorable is portable.

How beautiful would the world be if every human responded to Jesus' grace and loved God completely, themselves correctly, and their neighbors—of all ages and ethnicities—compassionately? We would have heaven on earth! The vision of Transformation Church, which is just God's vision for all of us, restores humanity to its original purpose for the glory of God. The vision of Transformation Church restores our humanity.

Remember, Jesus envisioned people living the Great Commandment and the Great Commission. He is the greatest vision caster of all! Transformation Church is a multiethnic local church because Jesus' vision commanded and demanded that it would be. Based on the Great Commandment and the Great Commission, I didn't think I had permission from Jesus to plant a homogeneous local church.

The Great Commandment and the Great Commission were the fuel that empowered the apostle Paul to plant multiethnic churches as well. But before Paul was a multiethnic church planter, he tried to destroy Jesus' church.

FROM CHURCH DESTROYER TO MULTIETHNIC CHURCH PLANTER

When I think of the word *grace,* a flood of emotions brings me to my knees in gratitude, because grace is not some dry, abstract theological concept. Grace is a person—Jesus—and I know him and he knows me. His love is better than life; he's utterly made me a new person.

Jesus himself is the unearned favor of God that makes the impossible possible. God the Father lavishly, through the Holy Spirit, indwells his people with the very life of Jesus so they can display the mind-blowing beauty of God's kingdom. The beauty of God's grace is seen in high definition when these words were written about Saul of Tarsus, who was transformed from a church destroyer into a multiethnic church planter:

> And I was still unknown in person to the churches of Judea that are in Christ. They only were hearing it said, "He who used to

persecute us is now preaching the faith he once tried to destroy."
And they glorified God because of me. (Galatians 1:22–24)

The early Jewish followers of the Messiah could not believe that the great persecutor of the church, Saul of Tarsus, was now preaching the very gospel that built Jesus' church. This is what the life-transforming beauty of God's grace can do. The impossible becomes the him-possible. Paul describes himself in this way:

> I too was convinced that I ought to do all that was possible to oppose the name of Jesus of Nazareth. And that is just what I did in Jerusalem. On the authority of the chief priests I put many of the Lord's people in prison, and when they were put to death, I cast my vote against them. Many a time I went from one synagogue to another to have them punished, and I tried to force them to blaspheme. I was so obsessed with persecuting them that I even hunted them down in foreign cities. (Acts 26:9–11 NIV)

Even while Saul persecuted the church, God, in his masterful orchestration of the universe, used him to build Jesus' multiethnic church even before he became a recipient of God's grace. Ultimately, the inspiration and motivation for the Apostle Paul to create multiethnic local churches was the Abrahamic covenant. For Paul, his mission to the Gentiles and the Jews was not a betrayal of the scripture, but its fulfilment (Galatians 3:8; Ephesians 2:12; Romans 15:5–13).

THE GREAT OMISSION BECOMES THE GREAT COMMISSION: ACTS 1:8; 8:1

The last words of someone are important, especially if that someone is the eternal Son, the second Person of the triune God. Before Jesus ascended to heaven so he could function as his people's great High Priest, he commissioned and commanded his twelve apostles (Acts 1:2) to be his "witnesses in Jerusalem and in all Judea and Samaria, and to the end of the earth" (Acts 1:8). These early Jewish believers disobeyed Jesus and his Great Commission by staying in Jerusalem among the Jews. They had a bad case of ethnocentrism, believing that the God of Abraham, Isaac, and Jacob was only for the Jews because God had given them the Law and circumcision as a badge of God's covenant. They forgot that, as Jews, they existed to be a light to the Gentiles.

But Jesus would not let them disrupt his mission to reach the Gentiles, fulfilling his promises to Abraham (see Genesis 12:1–3; Galatians 3:7–9; Romans 15:8–13). And, in order to force the homogeneous Jewish church in Jerusalem to scatter in this mission to reach the Gentiles, God allowed persecution to free the early Jewish church from the sin of ethnocentrism.

God used Saul and other enemies of the church to free it from the sin of not reaching the Gentiles and move it toward becoming multiethnic:

> And Saul approved of [Stephen's] execution. And there arose
> on that day a great persecution against the church in Jerusalem,

and they were all scattered throughout the regions of Judea and Samaria, except the apostles. Devout men buried Stephen and made great lamentation over him. But Saul was ravaging the church, and entering house after house, he dragged off men and women and committed them to prison. (Acts 8:1–3)

God is calling local churches in America and the world to be communities of unifiers and reconcilers, not dividers. Just as the church in Jerusalem only wanted to reach fellow Jews, the church in America is guilty of having ministry models that create homogeneous local churches. This is why nearly 90 percent of churches in America are made up of a single ethnicity. If the government, higher education, and corporations such as Google or Apple were as segregated as the church in America, there would a huge public outcry. Yet the church in America marches along, focused on "numerical growth over the biblical value of reconciliation and justice."[2]

Because of the gospel, God's new people in Christ Jesus bring unity and reconcile people. I love how God used the great church destroyer Saul to become the great multiethnic church planter.

FROM RACIST TO GRACIST[3]

As Paul traveled on his *mission* to arrest Jesus' disciples, he approached Damascus "breathing threats and murder against the disciples of the Lord" (Acts 9:1). But the Lord arrested him with grace (see Acts 9:1–19; 22:3–16; 26:4–18). I find it interesting that the name *Damascus* means "a sack full of blood."[4] Paul would go on to preach how the blood of Jesus not only washes people's sins but that his blood also creates a new humanity by reconciling and unifying

Jews and Gentiles. Look what Paul preached about Jesus' precious and beautiful blood and how it brought those who are "far"—that is, Gentiles—and those are "near"—namely, Jews—into a new humanity and new community called the church:

> But now in Christ Jesus you who once were far away have been brought near by the blood of Christ. . . . He came and preached peace to you who were far away and peace to those who were near. For through him we both have access to the Father by one Spirit. (Ephesians 2:13, 17–18 NIV)

Before King Jesus, the earth had two groups of humanity: Jews and Gentiles. After Jesus' resurrection, a third ethnicity was supernaturally born: the multicolored, multiethnic church. The church is not a weekend destination but a blood-bought, multicolored people.

As a result of Paul's encounter with the risen Lord Jesus, he would eventually give his life as a martyr so, as scholar N. T. Wright said, "cross-culturally united worship"[5] in the local church could be a reality and foretaste of God's eternal kingdom.[6] As a Pharisee, Saul was a rising rock star in this elite group of about seven thousand Jewish men tasked with keeping Israel religiously pure and in accord with God's laws. Saul, like many Jews in the first-century Greco-Roman world, potentially would have had contempt for Gentiles. For the majority of their existence, the Jewish people had experienced enslavement, racism, brutality, and oppression at the hands of Gentiles (including Egypt, Assyria, Babylon, Macedonia, and Rome).

Many Jews also viewed the Gentiles as religiously unclean because many of them were pagan idolaters who worshiped false gods through abominations like orgies and child sacrifices. If Gentiles were not God-fearers, which meant they believed in the one true God and denied the idols and foreign gods of the Gentile world, then many of the Jews would not have had much interaction with them religiously (see Acts 13:49–50; 17:4). God-fearers participated in the Jewish practices of tithing and regular prayers (see Acts 10:2–4). It is very likely they were welcome to take part in some synagogue services. God-fearers followed nearly every tenet of Judaism except circumcision.

Many Jews in the first-century Greco-Roman world believed that Gentiles were created to be fuel for the fires of hell. Some would not help a Gentile woman in the agony of childbirth because they would be guilty of helping her bring another Gentile into the world. If a Jew married a Gentile, the Jewish family would have a funeral for their Jewish son or daughter, and the Jewish child would be dead to the parents.[7] However, this doesn't mean the Jews totally separated themselves from Gentiles in everyday life; some types of everyday interaction would take place.

This horrible racism and ethnocentrism was not one-sided. Many Gentiles believed that Jews were less than human. For example, the Roman philosopher Cicero (106–43 BCE) wrote, "As the Greeks say, all men are divided into two classes—Greeks and barbarians. The Greeks called any man a barbarian who could not speak Greek; and they despised him and put up the barriers against him."[8]

The first-century world was filled with racism, sexism, division, injustice, and oppression. (Sounds a lot like the twenty-first century!) Paul said that Jews and Gentiles were divided by hostility and unreconciled (see Ephesians 2:14–16). But then Paul drops a gospel bomb on racism, hate, and division when he called Jesus our "peace." In a world saturated with hate, racism, and division, God brought peace in the Person of Jesus, and his peace is so beautiful that Jews and Gentiles, former enemies, would become a family and be a living example of God's invading the world with peace. The ethnic unity of God's church is a sign to the world that his kingdom has broken through the darkness.

The Story—Bigger, Greater, and More Beautiful

The book of Ephesians is breathtaking. Paul wrote this letter to the multiethnic congregations of Ephesus in modern-day Turkey. These ethnically diverse congregations of former enemies were struggling with getting along with each other as God's people (see Ephesians 4–5). It was out of pastoral concern that Paul wrote this letter to these Jewish-Gentile churches so they could be an expression of the glory of God by living in unity and love. The world would marvel, "How can enemies be friends now?" As churches, they would be living testimonies to God's grace. They would display to the world the beauty of reconciliation.

I propose that a primary reason the overwhelming majority of churches in America are homogeneous is because we've missed the beauty of why God the Holy Spirit authored the letter of Ephesians through Paul. And we've missed the beauty and purpose of Ephesians 2:8–9 by reducing it to an individualistic ticket to heaven: "For by grace you have been saved through faith. And this is not your own doing; it is the gift of God, not a result of works, so that no one may boast."

Exegetically, in his letter to the Ephesians, Paul taught something bigger, greater, and far more beautiful than just a trip to heaven when an individual Christ follower dies. In Ephesians 2:1, Paul said "you"—meaning the Gentiles—were spiritually dead people controlled by the devil and under God's impending judgment. But God, who is rich in mercy and love, made them alive with Christ, and they were saved by grace and seated in the heavenly realms with Christ (see Ephesians 2:1–6). In an act of incomprehensible grace, Gentiles were suddenly united to the Jewish Messiah; his life became their life. God performed this act of magnanimous love so he could point to the Gentiles (and Jews) as his trophies of grace for all eternity (see Ephesians 2:7).

Paul then said that it was by grace that the Gentiles were saved through faith in the Christ. This is the great gift in which no one can boast, but rather Jesus the Messiah did it all. Typically we stop there, but Paul didn't. He saw with gospel-vision the bigger, greater, and more beautiful story of what our triune God is accomplishing through the epic work and achievement of Jesus through his life, death, resurrection, and ascension.

In Ephesians 2:10, Paul wrote: "For we are God's handiwork, created in Christ Jesus to do good works, which God prepared in advance for us to do" (NIV). What are these good works the apostle spoke of that "God prepared in advance for us to do"? Based on Ephesians 2:11–22, these good works are the fulfillment of God's promises to Abraham in Genesis 12:1–3:

> Now the LORD said to Abram, "Go from your country and your kindred and your father's house to the land that I will show you.

And I will make of you a great nation, and I will bless you and make your name great, so that you will be a blessing. I will bless those who bless you, and him who dishonors you I will curse, and through you all the families of the earth shall be blessed."

God promised Abraham that all the families (both Jew and Gentile) on earth would be blessed through him. The great blessing is Jesus—the seed of Abraham—and through Jesus, a new multicolored family called the church would be blessed in him (see Ephesians 1:3–5). In Galatians 3:7–9 Paul wrote:

Know then that it is those of faith who are the sons of Abraham. And the Scripture, foreseeing that God would justify the Gentiles by faith, preached the gospel beforehand to Abraham, saying, "In you shall all the nations be blessed." So then, those who are of faith are blessed along with Abraham, the man of faith.

The heartbeat of salvation is that Jesus is faithful to his covenant with Abraham, and through his life, death, resurrection, and ascension, Jesus creates "in himself one new man in place of the two, so making peace, and might reconcile us both to God in one body through the cross, thereby killing the hostility" (Ephesians 2:15–16).

The bigger, greater, more gloriously beautiful story of salvation by grace through faith is that the God of heaven has created heavenly colonies of reconciliation and ethnic diversity on earth as it *will* be in heaven. N. T. Wright observed:

But whereas much western understanding has seen the individual as the goal, Paul sees individual Christians as signs pointing to a larger reality. He describes His own mission vividly in verse 20: We implore people on the Messiah's behalf, he writes, "to be reconciled to God." He longs to see the heaven-earth event, the temple event . . . the new temple is to be the place to which all nations will come to worship the God of Abraham and Jacob. . . . The reconciliation of Jews and Greeks was obviously near the heart of Paul's aim.[9]

In Ephesians 2:14–22, Paul dropped a series of explosive gospel bombs when he echoed words that call and empower God's people to live in unity. Paul said that this new multiethnic people made up of Jews and Gentiles has access to God the Father, are members of God's household and fellow citizens, and are God's dwelling place and temples (see Ephesians 2:17–22).

The gospel is about God's being faithful in Jesus to Abraham to colonize earth with his multiethnic, Jew-Gentile family, and this multiethnic family would be a living temple, God's dwelling place on earth. Wright added:

The larger reality, to which this points, the new creation itself, is to be symbolized by the whole church, united and holy. The new temple is to be the place to which all nations will come to worship the God of Abraham, Isaac, and Jacob. This is Paul's vision in the theological climax to the Romans in (15:7–12). . . . It was the vision of a new temple, a new house of praise, where songs originally sung in the shrine in Jerusalem would arise from hearts and mouths of every nation.[10]

In Romans 15:7–13 (NIV), Paul quotes several Old Testament scriptures to show it's always been God's heart to have a multiethnic church.

Accept one another, then, just as Christ accepted you, to bring praise to God. For I tell you that Christ has become a servant of the Jews on behalf of God's truth, so that the promise made to the patriarchs might be confirmed and, moreover, that the Gentiles might glorify God for his mercy. As it is written:

"Therefore I will praise you among the Gentiles;
I will sing the praises of your name." (Psalm 18:49)

Again, it says,

"Rejoice, you Gentiles, with his people."
(Deuteronomy 32:43)

And again,

"Praise the Lord, all you Gentiles
let all the peoples extol him." (Psalm 117:1)

And again, Isaiah says,

"The Root of Jesse will spring up,
one who will arise to rule over the nations;
in him the Gentiles will hope." (Isaiah 11:1, 10)

May the God of hope fill you with all joy and peace as you trust
in him, so that you may overflow with hope by the power of the
Holy Spirit. (Romans 15:7–13 NIV)

In light of this understanding, how could we not want to join
God in colonizing the earth with multiethnic congregations if the
demographics make it possible?

May Jesus raise up leaders who proclaim a gospel that creates
multiethnic local churches covering the face of not just America
but the world for the glory of God and as a sign and foretaste of the
coming great day!

AND THE WALLS CAME DOWN

Why is the church in America and throughout the world so segregated? It's because we've let tribalism, ethnocentrism, individualism,
consumerism, and classism create boundaries among God's people.
The Bible calls this sin.

I propose that God's people don't understand or believe deeply
enough in the bloody cross of Jesus and what his precious blood
accomplished. The bloody cross of Jesus breaks down the dividing walls killing the hostility between ethnic groups. It breaks my
heart to know that in 1912, the Church of God denomination, which
had roots in creating local multiethnic churches in the late 1800s,
split into Black and White denominations. In *United by Faith*, the
authors suggested, "An informal group of white leaders encouraged
African American leaders to establish their own national event. The

stated reason was that the large numbers of African Americans in attendance deterred whites from attending." The African Americans developed the National Association of the Church of God. How sad and how beneath the gospel, considering that early Church of God leaders, like a White pastor named Daniel S. Warner, "often defied segregation laws by holding interracial worship events."[11]

On a side note, the Church of God founded Anderson College in Anderson, Indiana, where I came to faith in a small dorm room on August 2, 1997. Also, William Seymour, a Black man and ordained Church of God minister, started the multiethnic Azusa Street Revival that birthed modern-day Pentecostalism. The Azusa Street Revival was national news because Blacks, Whites, Hispanics, Asians, and Native Americans all worshiped together.[12] In a time of racism and segregation, the gospel of grace broke down the walls of segregation and racism and birthed a reconciled and unified people. As Frank Bartleman, a minister in Los Angeles who witnessed the Azusa Street Revival, said, "The color line was washed away in the blood."[13]

The Azusa Street Revival began on April 9, 1906, the anniversary of which falls on my birthday. I wonder if it's more than coincidence that I came to faith at Anderson College, which was started by a denomination committed to planting multiethnic congregations, and that I was born on the day the multiethnic Azusa Street Revival began. Perhaps in the midst of one of those tongue-talking, tear-filled celebrations, people in those multiethnic gatherings were casting prayers into the heart of God that are now being poured out on me in my life and in this book.

Today's Pentecostal denominations emerged out of the multiethnic Azusa Street Revival. Sadly, these denominations, which started out as multiethnic, were "denominations split by race within a few years."[14]

The Temple's Dividing Wall

As a Pharisee, Paul knew about the dividing wall that separated Jews from Gentiles in the temple in Jerusalem. The temple campus was made up of a sequence of courts separated by gated walls. Each court moved closer to the Holy of Holies, where the presence of God dwelt. The gate of the Gentiles was the first gate through which God-fearing Gentiles were permitted to enter. Beyond that area, only Jewish men were permitted. Paul says that Jesus' bloody cross demolished the walls of separation and segregation. Jesus' blood is a bulldozer knocking over walls of division.

So, why is the church in America so segregated?

One of the reasons American churches are homogeneous is because we have erected walls and barriers caused by

1. racism (individually and structurally) and ethnocentrism,
2. the homogeneous unit principle (HUP), and
3. a small-minded, individualistic, underdeveloped view of the gospel.

Racism and Ethnocentrism Create Barriers

This one is pretty easy. Some Jesus followers are racist. I've had people tell me that Transformation Church is too ethnically diverse for them. In response I say, "Well, you aren't going to like the new heaven and the new earth at all because it will be way more beautiful and more diverse than Transformation Church."

In the multiethnic church at Antioch, Paul confronted the apostle Peter and rebuked him for his ethnocentrism (see Galatians 2:11-21). Paul said, "I opposed him to his face, because he stood condemned" (2:11) *Condemned* is a strong word! God condemns ethnocentrism and racism!

Before the Jews who were a part of the homogeneous church in Jerusalem arrived on an inspection tour in Antioch, Peter ate with Gentiles. After the Jerusalem Christians arrived, Peter "drew back and separated himself, fearing the circumcision party" (Acts 2:12). As the leader, Peter's sin caused the other Jews to dissociate from the Gentiles also. In essence, Paul said that ethnocentrism and racism was crucified on the cross! The racist I used to be is dead because the Messiah, the one who loved and gave himself for me, lives in me now (2:20). Therefore, Jews and Gentiles are of the same body and are equal because both have been justified (declared as righteous) by faith, not works of the law or Jewish ethnicity. God declares Jews and Gentiles righteous by grace because they have been incorporated into Christ.

We ourselves are Jews by birth and not Gentile sinners; yet we know that a person is not justified by works of the law but through faith in Jesus Christ, so we also have believed in Christ Jesus, in order to be justified by faith in Christ and not by works of the law, because by works of the law no one will be justified. . . .

I do not nullify the grace of God, for if righteousness were through the law, then Christ died for no purpose. (Galatians 2:15-16, 21)

The sad reality is that there are Jesus followers who believe their ethnic group is superior and their culture is better than others; therefore, they strategically target people in their own group and only that group to build churches. But the gospel of Jesus Christ will not tolerate this view. Listen to the one-time racist transformed into a gracist:

> For in Christ Jesus you are all sons of God, through faith. For as many of you as were baptized into Christ have put on Christ. There is neither Jew nor Greek, there is neither slave nor free, there is no male and female, for you are all one in Christ Jesus. And if you are Christ's, then you are Abraham's offspring, heirs according to promise. (Galatians 3:26–29)

The gospel makes us color-blessed, not color-blind. The cross births a new multiethnic people who define themselves by the color of Jesus' blood, not the color of their skin. The cross births a new people who view themselves as equals because they are reconciled to Christ and to one another. The bloody cross of Christ is now the driving force that influences us more than our culture. And once again Paul noted we are Abraham's offspring because God in Jesus is faithful to complete his promise to Abraham of creating a big, beautiful, multicolored family of unity and reconciliation. This gospel reality grips the heart of ministry leader. Keep in mind that individual racism is about negatively and often violently perceiving people of different ethnicities. But structural racism is about using power to suppress and oppress the other. Often, for the believers in the dominant culture, they are blind to structures that oppress others, but support them.

The Homogeneous Unit Principle Creates Barriers

The American church has gotten into bed with the homogeneous unit principle (HUP), and the offspring of this unholy union is ethnically, socioeconomically segregated congregations. In 1955, Donald McGavran's book *The Bridges of God* launched what we know today as the church growth movement. The HUP taught that "homogeneous churches grow faster because people prefer to attend church with those from similar racial, socioeconomic, ethnic and cultural backgrounds. In an attempt to draw individuals into church, barriers needed to removed, and that meant that dealing with racial differences which would detract from the real work of Church would not be considered."[15]

As a result of adherence to this principle, local church staffs are homogeneous. This lack of diversity is a huge barrier. Many of my White pastor friends ask me, "How come Black people won't come to our church, and if they do come, they don't stay?" My first response is, "Is your staff all White?" When they say they are, I explain, "That's a barrier." Having a homogeneous staff says only people like us can lead. And the same is true for my Black pastor friends.

Preaching a Small, Individualistic, Underdeveloped Gospel Creates Barriers

America is enslaved to individualism. Professor Soong-Chan Rah observed, "From the earliest stages of American history, individualism has been the defining attribute of our nation's ethos."[16] As a result, American Christians have been breast-fed and brought up on what I call the Gospel of Me. Instead of an individual existing for Jesus, Jesus exists to help an individual realize their potential and fulfill their dreams. Jesus is little more than a life coach. As a result of pastors being under the spell of individualism, the American church often preaches a small, individualistic gospel that focuses on getting people to heaven when they die instead of one that creates a redeemed, regenerated community that embodies the kingdom of God as God promised Abraham. Jesus, the King himself, blood-bought a Spirit-inhabited multiethnic church so it could be a foretaste of God's eternal church in the new heaven and the new earth here on earth (see Revelation 5:9–12).

ETHNICALLY DIVERSE LEADERSHIP TEAMS IN THE BOOK OF ACTS

If the leadership of the local church is not multiethnic, it's very unlikely that the church will be ethnically diverse. And if the church is diverse, your church leadership will be teaching the children of minorities that they are not fit to lead. They will see that people who share their ethnic background are not in leadership, influencing and shaping the direction of the church.

I knew that for Transformation Church to be intentionally multiethnic, our leadership team needed to reflect the diversity we wanted in our congregation. The early church did this also; this is where we got this leadership principle. In Acts 6:1–6 "a complaint by the Hellenists arose against the Hebrews because their widows were being neglected in the daily distribution." So the apostles asked seven godly Hellenistic Jews to share in the leadership. Look at the men's names: "What they said pleased the whole gathering, and they chose Stephen, a man full of faith and of the Holy Spirit, and

Philip, and Prochorus, and Nicanor, and Timon, and Parmenas, and Nicolaus, a proselyte of Antioch." All Greek names. This is gospel-shaped leadership in action.

In Acts 13, you see the same multiethnic church leaders shaped by a gospel-vision in practice. The church in Antioch was a multiethnic church that took the gospel to the world. Look at who comprises the leadership there: "Now there were in the church at Antioch prophets and teachers, Barnabas, Simeon who was called Niger, Lucius of Cyrene, Manaen, a lifelong friend of Herod the tetrarch, and Saul" (v. 1).

Simeon was from Niger, a country in sub-Saharan West Africa. Lucius of Cyrene was from a city near the northern coast of Africa in what is Libya today. Manaen was brought up with Herod the tetrarch, which mostly likely means he was born in Palestine with a wealthy, privileged upbringing. Barnabas was from Cyprus (see Acts 4:36), and Paul was from the Tarsus in Asia Minor (see Acts 9:1).[17] Luke, the author of Acts, led by God the Holy Spirit, reveals the gifting and the roles of the five leaders—the leadership team—of the multiethnic church at Antioch. Luke pointed out their ethnicity: two were from Africa, one was from the Mediterranean, one was from the Middle East, and one was from Asia Minor. The multiethnic church at Antioch was led by a multiethnic leadership team.

ETHNICALLY DIVERSE WORSHIP MUSIC

As a result of having a homogeneous staff, musical styles will cater to the likes of that group, creating another barrier to people who are not of the same ethnic background as the staff.

Music is important in building an ethnically diverse local

church. At Transformation Church, we first make sure that our worship music is Christ-exalting, that our stage is diverse, and that our sound is diverse. We've been able to develop our sound by not trying to sound like anyone. Our music was birthed out of a passion to reach a diverse community. You'll need to develop your own sound and find out what works for you in your context, but the way I see it, if Justin Timberlake has ethnically diverse concerts because his music is cross-cultural, the church can ethnically diversify worship services with cross-cultural music too.

No local church will be able to do this perfectly. Over the last five years I've learned to teach our congregation to serve one another by laying down musical preferences for the greater cause of building churches on earth that will look like the church in heaven. After a worship set, I say, "You know, for some of you, those songs may not have been your preference. But Jesus was exalted and some of your brothers and sisters loved it. Therefore, celebrate Jesus and celebrate them. Then next week they will do the same for you." When we lay down our preferences for a greater cause, we begin to serve each other, and when we serve each other, we are being Jesus to each other. Multiethnic local churches are built when we put down our preferences and pick up our crosses.

STUDY QUESTIONS, REFLECTIONS, AND PRAYER

1. Think through the following statement: a vision of the future transforms what you do today.

2. What is the vision of your church? Does that vision, if lived out, produce a gospel-centered, multiethnic church?

   a. What is the vision of Transformation Church and how was it formed? Discuss this as a team, or write down your thoughts.

   b. How can you communicate your vision more clearly?

3. How did God use persecution and Saul of Tarsus to move the Jewish church to fulfill Acts 1:8 and 8:1? Why didn't the Jewish church want to go to "Samaria" and to the ends of the earth?

4. What are the implications of this statement: "*Ministry leaders who are being formed into multiethnic church leaders realize that the ethnic unity of God's church is a sign to the world that his kingdom has broken through the darkness, establishing peace between enemies*"?

5. Read Ephesians 2:8–9. I write about how salvation is more than an "individualistic ticket to heaven." In what ways does reading these verses in light of God's covenant with Abraham affect your understanding of this passage? (Read Ephesians 2:10–13 and Genesis 12:1–3.)

6. Only 13 percent of churches today are considered multiethnic. What factors do you think influence the church to be homogeneous? What are some barriers you see in your church to creating a multiethnic, multiclass congregation? What can you do to change these?

PRAYER

Father, open our eyes so we may see the barriers that keep your people divided. Help me to see how structural racism suppresses and oppresses your precious children. Holy Spirit, give us courage to tear them down with the gospel. In Jesus' name, amen.

FOUR

SEEING CHRIST JESUS AND GOD'S ETERNAL PLAN

*And this is God's plan: Both Gentiles and
Jews who believe the Good News share equally
in the riches inherited by God's children. Both
are part of the same body, and both enjoy the
promise of blessings because they belong to Christ
Jesus. . . . This was his eternal plan, which he
carried out through Christ Jesus our Lord.*
—EPHESIANS 3:6, 11 NLT

THE TRANSFORMATION OF THE SNOTTY-NOSED RACIST

As I finished my closing prayer one Sunday, I noticed a White gentleman get up from his seat. I turned to greet and high-five some people, and the next thing I know, this guy is sprinting down the aisle toward me. As he is running, I see snot dangling from his nose and tears flooding down his face. In the next three seconds I had all kinds of crazy thoughts, including wondering if I would have to defend myself if this dude attacked me. Then I thought, *What would Jesus do? Well, for one thing, Jesus would do a miracle and make that snot disappear!* Before I knew it, we were face to face, and he was hugging me, snot and all. Then something amazing happened.

As he hugged me, he said, "I'm so glad someone invited me to this church. I never thought I'd ever be in church. Jesus is changing my life. And my pastor is Black! And I don't even like Black people!" Yep. You read that correctly. The White dude said, "And my pastor is Black! And I don't even like Black people!" So here's the scene: a Black pastor and a thirty-something White racist hugging in God's house. Yes, it was an *eptastic* (simultaneously epic and fantastic) moment.

Jesus transformed this White racist into a gracist. I still get goose bumps when I think of this moment. But more importantly, I experienced the power of Jesus and his cross that reconciles people unto himself and to each other.

Typically, when we study the life of Christ, we talk about Jesus being 100 percent God the Son and 100 percent man; we talk about him being the ultimate Prophet, Priest, and King; we talk about his birth, sinless life, death, resurrection, and ascension, but we seldom talk about how Jesus, Israel's Messiah, created a new ethnicity of people of Jews and Gentiles through his finished work and how this new ethnicity is called God's church.

The apostle Paul wrote:

And this is God's plan: Both Gentiles and Jews who believe the Good News share equally in the riches inherited by God's children. Both are part of the same body, and both enjoy the promise of blessings because they belong to Christ Jesus. . . . This was his eternal plan, which he carried out through Christ Jesus our Lord. (Ephesians 3:6, 11 NLT)

Jesus carried out God's plan; therefore, I am more determined, more committed in my pursuit of building a healthy, thriving multiethnic church and helping other pastors and denominational leaders do likewise, because the local church is God's grand prototype that displays to the world how humanity is to love one another. The power of Jesus' cross is greater than the power of racism. As an illustration of this statement, let me give you the backstory of the racist-turned-gracist.

THE BACKSTORY

A few months before Austin ran down the aisle, a woman who was a member of Transformation Church invited Austin's girlfriend, Amber, to one of our Easter services. The Spirit opened Amber's broken heart as the gospel of grace was preached. Amber received Jesus as God and King that Easter.

Before Amber was at Transformation Church, she had spent four years in prison for various crimes. When she was a little girl, her father and other relatives, male and female, physically and sexually abused her. During her teenage years, her family disowned her. In high school, Amber experimented with marijuana and then progressed to alcohol, crack, and, finally, to heroin. To support her addiction she became a stripper and prostitute.

After her stint in prison, Amber met Austin. He came from

a middle-class Midwestern family. Growing up, he had everything he needed, but in high school, he, too, started smoking weed, which led to harder drugs like heroin. When Austin and Amber met, they both were a mess. And in the midst of their mess, God sent a missionary from Transformation Church into their lives.

After that Easter service, Amber became a regular attender at Transformation Church, but Austin refused to go hear a "n—preacher!" But Austin couldn't argue with how Amber's life was rapidly transforming. Finally, Austin agreed to come to a service, and Jesus wrecked him. I baptized both Amber and Austin the following Easter.

As Austin and I grew in our friendship, I asked why he had resisted attending a service with Amber. He said, "Because I didn't like Black people, and I expected you to be shuckin' and jivin.'" (I have no idea what shuckin' and jivin' is.) Then he said, "I tried with everything in me not to like you or your sermon, but the more you preached, the more I felt God's love touch my heart in places I didn't even know I had. At the end of the sermon, I just knew I wanted Jesus."

After a year or so of being faithful participants of Transformation Church, Austin and Amber approached me to ask me if I would perform their wedding. The Transformation Church care team took them through a premarital counseling class. As we approached the wedding date, Amber asked me a beautiful question: "Pastor Derwin, my father is not in my life. He disowned me a long time ago. Would you please walk me down the aisle and give me away?" In an intimate gathering, I walked Amber down the aisle, and with each step we could see the tears streaming down Austin's face. It was a great honor to give Amber away to Austin and to officiate their wedding.

Amber and Austin became passionate missionaries and super servant-leaders at Transformation Church. Amber went on to get a master's degree, and they both are sober and have great jobs. I believe Austin and Amber's story is a microcosm of God's heart for his church and how the work of Christ not only forgives people but makes them into a new people where hostilities are put to death (see Ephesians 2:16). The local church exists to be a community of healing and reconciliation. Healing from all kinds of sins like sexual abuse, drug abuse, and racism. But how can racists ever get transformed into gracists in homogeneous churches?

MESS TO MASTERPIECE

The local church is a community of grace where messed-up people become masterpieces. As Paul wrote, "For we are his workmanship, created in Christ Jesus for good works, which God prepared beforehand, that we should walk in them" (Ephesians 2:10). In Christ Jesus, we are God's workmanship, or new creation. Another way to say it is that, in Christ, we are a new ethnicity comprised of Jews and Gentiles who are created to do the good things God planned long ago.

According to Paul:

For Christ himself has brought peace to us. He united Jews and Gentiles into one people when, in his own body on the cross, he broke down the wall of hostility that separated us. He did this by ending the system of law with its commandments and regulations. He made peace between Jews and Gentiles by creating in himself one new people from the two groups. (Ephesians 2:14–15 NLT)

It's as if Jesus rained down peace as his blood fell from the rugged cross. This precious, divine blood created a new multiethnic people. These new people of God are reconciled with God the Papa and reconciled with one another, producing local multiethnic churches progressively moving toward reconciliation, healing, and love.

God's heart's desire for Jews and Gentiles to love each other and be reconciled to one another didn't start in the first-century Greco-Roman world. It has been God's heartbeat—the rhythm of his dance—for all eternity.

The Dance-with-Me God

The God of Abraham, Isaac, and Jacob is a tripersonal being. The apostle John revealed a magnificent truth about the tripersonal God when he said, "God is love" (1 John 4:8). As we pull back the curtains of eternity, we learn that God has never been alone. God has always been a dynamic, interactive community of love. God the Father is the lover, God the Son is the beloved, and God the Holy Spirit is the spirit of love. Love demands relationship; therefore, God's nature as a tripersonal being makes him eternally love.

But the God of the Bible is also a dancing God. Once again, the apostle John helps us see a beautiful, eternal truth when he wrote,

"In the beginning was the Word, and the Word was with God, and the Word was God" (John 1:1).

The word *with* in Greek as used in John 1:1 is *pro*, meaning "to move toward." This word implies a face-to-face relationship. It's a term of deep intimacy. I like to say intimacy means "into me you see." The early Greek fathers of the church also had a word for this: *perichoresis*. From all eternity, God the Father, God the Son, and God the Holy Spirit loved, adored, and rejoiced in one another.[1]

From all eternity the tripersonal God has danced the dance of love, and out of his measureless, bottomless, boundless love, the tripersonal God created image bearers named Adam and Eve. When God created them, it was as if he said, "Will you dance with me? And because my life is in you, your children will dance with me, and one day all the people on earth will dance with me too."

God, not out of need but out of love, fashioned Adam and Eve in his image to represent his limitless love throughout the earth. God desired that humanity would dance the dance of love with him and with one another. Earth was to be God's dance floor where his image bearers would simply love him and one another. Earth would be a miniversion of heaven. But instead of earth becoming God's dance floor, it has become his battlefield.

Why Did Adam and Eve Stop Dancing with God?

Adam and Eve decided they didn't want to dance with God anymore, and they chose to dance with the serpent instead. The serpent played some rhythmic, intoxicating music that captured their affections. They liked the sound so much, they stopped dancing with God and died. They fell off the dance floor, and so did all their offspring (see Romans 5:12–14).

But God invites all humanity to dance with him again. God played his beautiful eternal melody, and a pagan named Abram heard it and decided to dance with God. This music God played was the gospel. God preached the gospel to Abram before Peter, James, John, and Paul were ever born when he said:

> Go from your country and your kindred and your father's house to the land that I will show you. And I will make of you a great nation, and I will bless you and make your name great, so that you will be a blessing. I will bless those who bless you, and him who dishonors you I will curse, and in you all the families of the earth shall be blessed. (Genesis 12:1–3)

Does it surprise you that God preached the gospel to Abram before the apostles?

The Gospel Preached to Abraham

Pastor, church planter, leader, don't miss this essential gospel reality that the apostle Paul reaffirmed when he wrote under the inspiration of the Holy Spirit: "And the Scripture, foreseeing that God would justify the Gentiles by faith, preached the gospel beforehand to Abraham, saying, 'In you shall all the nations be blessed.' So then, those who are of faith are blessed along with Abraham, the man of faith" (Galatians 3:8–9).

So, through Abram, whom God renamed Abraham, meaning

"father of many," all the families (ethnic groups) on earth would be blessed by the gospel and be included in Abraham's family through faith in Jesus of Nazareth, Israel's Messiah. Humanity would be able to dance the dance of love with God and one another. Through Abraham, the nation of Israel was birthed, and they corporately had the sacred vocation of being a "light to the Gentiles" (see Isaiah 42:6; 49:6; 51:4; 60:3).

Israel, however, failed in this task just as Adam failed before them. God in his omniscience knew that, which is why Jesus was slain before the world began (see Revelation 13:8; Ephesians 1:4–5). That was Jesus already on his way to save us. Before we ever called his name, he was already coming to rescue us.

PAUL'S PASSION FOR DIVERSITY

Through Jesus, the church now becomes the light of the world to reach those in darkness with the gospel message: "'In you shall all the nations be blessed'" (Galatians 3:8). And Paul, a leader captured by God's gospel vision, was convinced that local multiethnic churches were God's covenantal fulfillment to Abraham (see Ephesians 2:14–22; Galatians 3:7–14). God saves people individually and transforms their lives for the purpose of creating local multiethnic churches that function as communities of reconciliation and unity.

To show Paul's passion for multiethnic churches, look at how many times in his letters he talked about Jewish and Gentile local churches.

PAUL'S PASSION IN ROME

In the first chapter of Romans, Paul wrote:

> Through whom we have received grace and apostleship to bring
> about the obedience of faith for the sake of his name among all
> the nations. . . .
>
> I do not want you to be unaware, brothers, that I have often
> intended to come to you (but thus far have been prevented), in
> order that I may reap some harvest among you as well as among
> the *rest of the Gentiles*. I am under obligation both to *Greeks and
> to barbarians*, both to the wise and to the foolish. So I am eager
> to preach the gospel to you also who are in Rome.
>
> For I am not ashamed of the gospel, for it is the power of God
> for salvation to everyone who believes, to the Jew first and also to
> the Greek. (1:5, 13–16, emphasis added)

Paul said he was under an obligation to reach all people: Jews,
Greeks, and barbarians. In my context in the area around Charlotte,
North Carolina, there are White people, Black people, Asian people,
Latino people, and people who are ethnically mixed. The gospel
demands, it obliges me, to intentionally reach all people. Therefore,
because of the gospel, Transformation Church and I are under an
obligation to preach God's message and create a ministry culture
that is inclusive of ethnically diverse people. We can't do this perfectly, but we can do the best we can.

The apostle Paul's passion to join Jesus in building diverse local
churches was on display in Corinth, a rough and gritty diverse
urban setting.

PAUL'S PASSION IN CORINTH

In 1 Corinthians, Paul wrote:

For though I am free from all, I have made myself a servant to all, that I might win more of them. To the Jews I became as a Jew, in order to win Jews. To those under the law I became as one under the law (though not being myself under the law) that I might win those under the law. To those outside the law I became as one outside the law (not being outside the law of God but under the law of Christ) that I might win those outside the law. To the weak I became weak, that I might win the weak. I have become all things to all people, that by all means I might save some. *I do it all for the sake of the gospel* that I may share with them in its blessings.

Do you not know that in a race all the runners run, but only one receives the prize? So run that you may obtain it. (9:19–24, emphasis added)

In Corinth, Paul says that, for the sake of the gospel, he reached Jews and Gentiles and planted multiethnic churches. For the apostle, building multiethnic churches was a gospel issue. This was the race Paul ran. Pastor, are you running a race that will produce a homogeneous local church? Is your staff representative of only one ethnic group? Is your preaching and music fitted for one specific kind of people? Are you cross-culturally incompetent? If you answered yes to these questions, you are not running the same race the apostle Paul ran. Leaders compelled by a gospel vision of love, grace, and reconciliation are committed to running the race the apostle Paul ran.

Let's now learn from Paul in Galatia.

PAUL'S PASSION IN GALATIA

To the believers in Galatia, Paul wrote, "For as many of you as were baptized into Christ have put on Christ. There is neither Jew nor Greek, there is neither slave nor free, there is no male and female, for you are all one in Christ Jesus. And if you are Christ's, then you are Abraham's offspring, heirs according to promise" (Galatians 3:27–29).

The gospel Paul preached was a deep gospel that went beyond just saving souls to building heavenly, barrier-breaking communities of reconciliation. The gospel Paul preached destroyed racism ("neither Jew no Greek"), economic classism ("slave nor free"), and gender inequality ("no male and female"). The local church should be a mosaic that the world looks at and says, "So that's what heaven looks like."

In Ephesus, Paul's passion to see heaven on earth is amplified!

PAUL'S PASSION IN EPHESUS

To the churches in Ephesus, Paul wrote, "This mystery is that the Gentiles are fellow heirs, members of the same body, and partakers of the promise in Christ Jesus through the gospel. Of this gospel I was made a minister according to the gift of God's grace, which was given me by the working of his power" (Ephesians 3:6–7).

Paul says that the mystery of Christ is that Jews and Gentiles are of the same body and are partakers of the "promise," which is the promise of the Abrahamic covenant that was fulfilled through Jesus and the gospel. Then he says that he is a minister of this gospel and empowered by the Holy Spirit to build multiethnic local churches like the ones in Ephesus. Pastor, are you preaching Paul's gospel, a gospel that unites and reconciles ethnically diverse people? Sadly, pastors have told me they are called to target a certain ethnic group or class of people.

Let's now see Paul's passion in his letter to the churches at Philippi.

PAUL'S PASSION IN PHILIPPI

In Philippi, one of Paul's multiethnic local churches was under attack by Judaizers, whom Paul called "dogs" and "evildoers" and "those who mutilate the flesh" (Philippians 3:2). The issue at hand was ethnocentrism. If the Gentiles wanted to really follow the Jewish Messiah, the Judaizers said they must embrace a Jewish identity through circumcision. Paul's message was that it was grace and the work of Jesus that saved them, not being ethnically Jewish or by works of the Law. Paul dealt with this same issue in Galatia: "For neither circumcision counts for anything, nor uncircumcision, but a new creation" (Galatians 6:15).

When we first came to Christ, my wife and I joined a homogeneous megachurch. Even though the area around the church was ethnically diverse, the congregation was not. The pastor and people of this church loved us, and we loved them. The leadership, the music, and the culture were geared toward the White middle-class majority culture. In essence, this culture said that you could belong to this church if we can assimilate you to become like us. It was a form of ethnocentrism birthed not out of evil intent but simple ignorance. Most churches don't even realize they are doing this because it's become such an ingrained pattern in the American church.

In Colossi, we see a similar pattern and passion from the apostle Paul.

Paul's Passion in Colossi

To the multiethnic churches at Colossi, Paul wrote, "Here there is not Greek and Jew, circumcised and uncircumcised, barbarian, Scythian, slave, free; but Christ is all, and in all" (Colossians 3:11). Why did Paul need to write this letter to this young church? He wrote because the different ethnic groups were not getting along. They were fighting. The sins of racism, ethnocentrism, and classism were causing hurt, conflict, and division.

The Colossi churches had Greeks, Jews, barbarians, Scythians, slaves, and free people. It was ethnically and socioeconomically diverse. It's important to note that the term *Greek* did not necessarily refer to a specific ethnic group but rather to a community of people who spoke the same language and embraced Greek culture. Greeks called anyone they considered uncultured or who didn't speak Greek "barbarians." It's a derogatory term. A Scythian was someone from the Black Sea tribes.[2] The term *Scythian* was even worse than being called a barbarian. And Paul had heard that these believers were referring to each other by their old identities, which caused pain and conflict. There were also two classes of people in this church: slave and free. Slaves and indentured servants would have been comparable to the poor, and the free would be like the middle class today. In his letter to these churches, Paul showed how the gospel eradicates racism, ethnocentrism, and classism. He

longed for God's people to see themselves as God's new humanity defined by Israel's Messiah, not their skin colors, cultures, or
wealth. Ethnic and cultural differences are not obliterated; they
are embraced. What are obliterated are the barriers that divide us.
There is no favored ethnicity, class, or gender in God's church; we
are equal in Christ, thus we are equally beloved. Paul's theology was
radical in the first-century Greco-Roman world because it flew in
the face of traditional cultural norms.

We see this gospel principle at work in Paul's letter to the
Colossians:

> Put on then, as God's chosen ones, holy and beloved, compassion-
> ate hearts, kindness, humility, meekness, and patience, bearing
> with one another and, if one has a complaint against another, for-
> giving each other; as the Lord has forgiven you, so you also must
> forgive. And above all these put on love, which binds everything
> together in perfect harmony. And let the peace of Christ rule in
> your hearts, to which indeed you were called in one body. And
> be thankful. Let the word of Christ dwell in you richly, teaching
> and admonishing one another in all wisdom, singing psalms and
> hymns and spiritual songs, with thankfulness in your hearts to
> God. And whatever you do, in word or deed, do everything in the
> name of the Lord Jesus, giving thanks to God the Father through
> him. (3:12–17)

If we really want to be faithful to the text, then we must follow Paul's admonitions to the multiethnic church in Colossi about
embodying the kingdom of God. Leading a multiethnic church is

difficult, but it is so worth it to the people who are transformed as a result of engaging and interacting with people vastly different from them.

MORE THAN MEETS THE EYE

We see this gospel leadership reality in none other than Jesus himself. In John 4, Jesus and his disciples do the unthinkable: they travel through Samaria. Jews avoided Samaria like people avoid a quarantined area. Samaritans and Jews hated each other. They despised each other's ethnicity, religions, and cultures. But their hate for one another didn't stop Jesus from reaching his divine appointment with a woman at a well.

The woman at the well shows up at noon, which is an indicator that she wanted to avoid the other Samaritan women who would have gone to the well in the cool of the morning or the early evening to fetch water. She had a messed-up past. She had been through five divorces and was living with a man who was not her husband. She was a social outcast. Samaritans rejected her based on her past, and Jews would have rejected her for her ethnicity and religious practices. But Jesus accepted her. And in his experience with the woman at the well, we discover something beautiful.[3] What is a Samaritan woman? She has a mixed Jewish and Gentile ethnicity; she was a Jew and a Gentile in one body. In the Samaritan woman, we get a picture of how the church universally and locally is one body, mixed with Jews and Gentiles. The apostle Paul said: "He made peace between Jews and Gentiles by creating in himself one new people from the two groups. Together as one body, Christ reconciled both groups to God by means of his death on the cross, and our hostility toward each other was put to death" (Ephesians 2:15–16 NLT).

Jesus rejected the status quo and ran toward the other, regardless of cultural norms. How about you, pastor? Are you ready to preach a gospel that reaches the "other"? Are you ready to create ministry environments that are welcoming and inclusive to all? My friend Matt Chandler, lead pastor of The Village Church and president of Acts 29, wrote, "In the past few years, I have come to realize that planting and growing homogeneous churches can be done with relative ease and a lack of dependence of the Spirit."[4]

THE FIRST MAJOR CHURCH DISPUTE

In Acts 15, we find the first major church dispute. Considering how Christians like to argue, the reason for the disagreement is quite interesting. Was it over Calvinism? Arminianism? Molinism? Was it over speaking in tongues? prophecy? healing? Maybe it was over worship music styles and Jews who couldn't accept the Greek worship leaders wearing tight, skinny-leg jeans.

Actually, the first major church dispute was over how fast multiethnic churches were growing outside of Jerusalem. These ethnically diverse congregations were blowing up the mental and cultural circuits of the Jewish believers in the holy city. These first-century multiethnic churches included Jews and Gentiles of Phoenicia and Samaria as well as uncircumcised Africans, Arabs, Greeks, Syrians, Asians, Romans, Persians, and more. Their presence and growth challenged the traditional concepts of what it meant to be Jewish and what it meant to follow Jesus.

Theologian Christopher J. H. Wright summarized the disagreement in this way:

> If only all the theological disputes in Christian history had been caused by successful mission and rapid church growth. Undoubtedly the first dispute was. The first major council of the church (Acts 15) was convened to consider a knot of problems caused by the success of cross-cultural church planting efforts. These had been initiated by the church of Antioch and carried out among the predominately Gentile and ethnically diverse peoples of the Roman provinces that made up what we now call Turkey. Paul and Barnabas, who had been entrusted with this initiative, were not the first to cross the barrier from Jew to Gentile with the good news of Jesus Christ. Philip (Act 8) and Peter (Acts 10) had already done that. They were, however, the first to establish whole communities of believers from mixed Jewish and Gentile backgrounds—that is, to plant multiethnic churches.[5]

Luke, Paul's Gentile traveling companion, wrote:

> But some men came down from Judea and were teaching the brothers, "Unless you are circumcised according to the custom of Moses, you cannot be saved." And after Paul and Barnabas had no small dissension and debate with them, Paul and Barnabas and some of the others were appointed to go up to Jerusalem to the apostles and the elders about this question. So, being sent on their way by the church, they passed through both Phoenicia and Samaria, describing in detail the conversion of the Gentiles,

and brought great joy to all the brothers. When they came to Jerusalem, they were welcomed by the church and the apostles and the elders, and they declared all that God had done with them. But some believers who belonged to the party of the Pharisees rose up and said, "It is necessary to circumcise them and to order them to keep the law of Moses." (Acts 15:1–5)

During the first century, there were several streams of thought concerning the salvation and inclusion of the Gentiles into Israel, from the destruction of the Gentiles, to the Gentiles coming to worship God without proselytism, to Gentiles making a pilgrimage to worship the one true God.

Specifically, converted Pharisees responded to the news about the growing churches from Paul and Barnabas by saying, "It is necessary to circumcise them and to order them to keep the law of Moses" (Acts 15:5). They leaned on their ethnicity as the means for their salvation and coupled it with belief in the Jewish Messiah. Their thinking was that the Jews were God's chosen people. It was Jews who had the Law, the Sabbath, and circumcision. Therefore, Gentiles had to become Jews in order to become saved and to become members of God's people. This is called ethnocentrism.

In the midst of this heated debate, Peter said:

Brothers, you know that in the early days God made a choice among you, that by my mouth the Gentiles should hear the word of the gospel and believe. And God, who knows the heart, bore witness to them, by giving them the Holy Spirit just as he did to us, and he made no distinction between us and them, having cleansed their hearts by faith. Now, therefore, why are you put-ting God to the test by placing a yoke on the neck of the disciples that neither our fathers nor we have been able to bear? But we believe that we will be saved through the grace of the Lord Jesus, just as they will. (Acts 15:7–11)

Peter's words match Paul's letter to the Galatians: "For as many of you as were baptized into Christ have put on Christ. There is nei-ther Jew nor Greek, there is neither slave nor free, there is no male and female, for you are all one in Christ Jesus. And if you are Christ's, then you are Abraham's offspring, heirs according to promise" (3:27–29). To Paul, it was not ethnicity or works of the Law that saved the Jews or Gentiles. It was the life, death, resurrection, and ascension of Israel's Messiah alone. Jews would still get circumcised, and they would get baptized as a sign of the covenant, but it was the work of the Messiah that saved them and brought them into a new family. Gentiles would simply be baptized as a sign of the covenant.

At the Jerusalem Council, Paul and Barnabas shared the great work that Jesus was doing among the Gentiles, and the assembly fell silent (see Acts 15:12). They were gripped by the grace of God. James, the leader of the Jerusalem church, declared that it had always been God's heart for the Gentiles to know him and be included in Abraham's family. James knew that Gentile inclusion was the ful-fillment of the Abrahamic covenant (see Acts 15:15–17). And he finished with these words:

Therefore my judgment is that we should not trouble those of the Gentiles who turn to God, but should write to them to abstain from the things polluted by idols, and from sexual immorality, and from what has been strangled, and from blood. For from ancient generations Moses has had in every city those who proclaim him, for he is read every Sabbath in the synagogues. (Acts 15:19–21)

In the first church dispute, James says no to Jewish ethnocentrism and yes to Christocentrism and grace. The Gentiles were encouraged to reject their former way of life, which included food polluted by idols and sexual immortality, and to abstain from eating the meat of strangled animals and their blood.

Sure, the Jerusalem Council in Acts 15 was about circumcision and food, but it was also about ethnicity. The gospel of grace is so glorious—a new humanity is created and people are reconciled to God and to one another (see 2 Corinthians 5:14–21). Before Jesus, there were two ethnic groups on earth: Jew and Gentile. After Jesus' resurrection, a new ethnic group made up of Jews and Gentiles was birthed. This new ethnic group is called the church—the "one new man" (see Ephesians 2:14–16).

In the twenty-first-century American church and in the world, these concepts of circumcision and eating restrictions do not mean much, but when we build homogeneous local churches, even though ethnic diversity is possible, it is a form of ethnocentrism. Homogeneous churches essentially promote a culture that says, "Our way of being the church is better than your way, and that's why our ministry models are geared to reach and minister to people who are like the majority culture that make up our church." I suspect this is mostly done out of ignorance, not malicious intent.

For example, my daughter's former high school was 60 percent White and 40 percent Black, Asian, and Latino, and mixed ethnicities. Yet every church in this area is overwhelmingly homogeneous. We hide our ethnocentrism with excuses like "This is our style" or "This is the way we've always done church." The gospel of the Lord Jesus doesn't give us the option to build homogeneous local churches, because God desires for local churches to reflect the eternal church.

WE NEED SOME COURAGEOUS PIONEERS

Now, I want to turn our attention to the church at Antioch. This church, like every church outside of Jerusalem, was a multiethnic church. And this church sent the gospel around the world. The church at Antioch should be the model for every local multiethnic church on the face of the planet.

The city of Antioch was established by Seleucus I, one of Alexander the Great's generals, near the end of the fourth century BCE. It was the third largest city in the Roman Empire with a population of eight hundred thousand. Antioch was segregated into two primary sections, one for Syrians and one for Greeks. The original settlement was comprised of retired soldiers from Seleucus's Macedonian army, Cretans, Cypriots, Argives, Herakleuda, Athenians from Atigona, and Jews from nearby Palestine, slaves of diverse ethnic origins, and native Syrians. And as a result, Antioch was fractured into numerous ethnic ghettos.

During the days of Roman rule in 64 BCE, the city attracted Gauls, Germans, and other barbarians. The population was divided into eighteen tribes throughout the city. As a result of ethnic divisions and an influx of newcomers, as with most cities of the era,

Antioch was prone to race riots.[6] And into this ethnically divided city, Jesus raised a church here that sent the gospel out to the world! In this ethnically fractured, divided city, Jews and Gentiles formed a community around the Jewish Messiah and his gospel of grace. Jesus' multiethnic church in Antioch displayed to the city what love, reconciliation, and unity looked like. People who were once divided were now unified in Christ. And I believe the same Holy Spirit that birthed the multiethnic church in Antioch can do it again in the United States today (see Acts 11:19–26; 13:1–3; Galatians 2:11–21).

HOW DID THE CHURCH AT ANTIOCH GET STARTED?

Who were the missionary church planters that ventured into this ethnically divided, volatile city and proclaimed Jesus and his grace? In Acts 11:19–21, we are told:

> Now those who were scattered because of the persecution that arose over Stephen traveled as far as Phoenicia and Cyprus and Antioch, speaking the word to no one except Jews. But there were some of them, men of Cyprus and Cyrene, who on coming to Antioch spoke to the Hellenists [Greeks] also, preaching the Lord Jesus. And the hand of the Lord was with them, and a great number who believed turned to the Lord.

Let's look at this and do a little review. Jesus commissioned his disciples to make disciples of all nations (people from all ethnic backgrounds) in Matthew 28:18–20 and Acts 1:8. Jesus wanted his disciples to preach the gospel to the Gentiles. As we see from the book of Acts, they refused to do this and were disobedient. For these early Jewish followers of Jesus, they simply wanted to build homogeneous churches for other Jews. In order to move his people toward the mission to build Jesus' multiethnic church, Jesus allowed persecution to arise, forcing them to leave Jerusalem and enter lands where Gentiles lived.

Don't these early disciples sound like the church today? We only produce ministry models that reach people who look like us. Remember, local churches are ten times more segregated than their neighborhoods and twenty times more segregated than the schools in their area.[7] I wonder if Jesus will allow persecution of the church in America and around the world so we can move out of our ethnocentric ghettos and become missionaries to all the people around us, not just people who are like us.

In Acts 11:20–21, something beautiful and supernatural happened, namely, some courageous, nameless "men of Cyprus and Cyrene" decided to obey Jesus and preach to the Greeks (Hellenists). And from these unknown men who loved Jesus and had a passion for all ethnic groups to love Jesus, the great church of Antioch was birthed. Perhaps the nameless men who broke down the ethnic barriers and preached the gospel to Greeks were Lucius of Cyrene, an African and one of the prophets and teachers at Antioch (Acts 13:1), and Barnabas, a native of Cyprus (Acts 4:36). Whoever these first-century disciples were, they inspire me and should be a model for us to follow. They rejected the status quo. They rejected ethnocentrism.

They rejected fear. They obeyed Jesus and took the gospel to others. These courageous pioneers rejected the homogeneous unity principle. Today, the American church needs some courageous pioneers who are fueled by the Spirit of God, the heart of God, and the glory of God to spread the gospel to all people, so all will know his Son Jesus, so the earth can be filled with multiethnic churches that reflect the future eternal church.

Paul Got His Start in Antioch

Luke wrote, "So Barnabas went to Tarsus to look for Saul, and when he had found him, he brought him to Antioch. For a whole year they met with the church and taught a great many people. And in Antioch the disciples were first called Christians" (Acts 11:25–26).

It was to the multiethnic church at Antioch that Barnabas brought Paul to experience the grace of God. It was in a large, urban, ethnically divided city that Paul became infected with God's passion for the local church to be gospel-centered, missional, and multiethnic. It was at this beautiful, multicolored church at Antioch that the Holy Spirit tattooed Paul's heart with the beauty, wonder, and power of multiethnic churches.

Think about this: Barnabas most likely started the multiethnic church in Antioch, yet it was the man he brought from Tarsus, Paul, who ends up writing over 60 percent of the New Testament and is known as the champion of multiethnic churches. Barnabas must have known Paul would be gifted enough to take the movement to the next level.

THE DISCIPLES WERE FIRST CALLED CHRISTIANS
AT ANTIOCH

Can you imagine how the racially divided people of Antioch looked at the integrated church in their city? Can you imagine how puzzled they must have been? They were so amazed, they called these reconciled and unified people "Christians."

Perhaps an ethnically divided, cynical twenty-first-century world would call us Christians if they see local churches become communities of love, reconciliation, and unity. The church in America and across the world is in desperate need of a new kind of missionary that builds a new kind of local church, which is actually an ancient kind of church: multiethnic local churches. I would say the New Testament knows nothing of a homogeneous local church other than the churches in Jerusalem.

Jesus, Israel's Messiah, realized God's plan of making a new humanity out of Jews and Gentiles to create a multicolored people called the church.

Are you this new kind of missionary church planter? Are you a ministry shaped by a gospel vision of love, grace, and reconciliation? I believe you can be.

STUDY QUESTIONS, REFLECTIONS,
AND PRAYER

1. Think through the following statement: *"Gospel-shaped leaders are committed to a gospel that creates local churches where the walls of hostility are broken down by the power of God's peace, reconciliation, and love."*

2. When did God preach the gospel to Abraham? Read Genesis 12:1–3 and Galatians 3:7–9. What does this mean for your understanding of the gospel?

3. Discuss the apostle Paul's passion to plant and build multi-ethnic local churches. Read Romans 1:5, 14; 1 Corinthians 9:19–22; Galatians 3:24–29; Ephesians 2:14–16; 3:6–7; and Colossians 3:11. What does Paul say about the people in these churches? What are the implications?

4. *"Gospel-formed leaders are committed to a deep gospel that goes beyond just saving souls to building heavenly, barrier-breaking communities of reconciliation."* In what ways did Paul reflect this commitment? What are the implications of this for you and your church?

5. Read Acts 11:19–26. How was the church at Antioch founded? What principles can you draw from the multiethnic church at Antioch?

PRAYER

Father, through the life, death, resurrection, and ascension of Jesus and the sealing work of the Spirit, bless and empower each of us to be a leader who is committed to a gospel that creates local churches where the walls of hostility are broken down by the power of your peace, reconciliation, and love. In Jesus' name, amen.

FIVE

SEEING MISSIONALLY AND RECONCILIATIONALLY

*And he said to me, "Go, for I will send
you far away to the Gentiles."*
—ACTS 22:21

WHY DO WE DO WHAT WE DO?

My Christian brothers and sisters confuse me at times. I don't think we think theologically or missiologically enough about why we live and do ministry the way we do. I don't understand why my White brothers and sisters in Christ will go all the way to Africa on short-term mission trips to preach the gospel across the sea to Black people, yet many of the local churches they attend are not intentionally trying to reach the Black people who live across the street.

Several times a month, when I'm out and about in my neighborhood, many of my White brothers and sisters in Christ who do not attend Transformation Church have said to me, "Pastor Derwin, I recommended a family to your church. They were looking for a racially diverse church, so I told them about Transformation." I politely thank them, but then sadness overwhelms me, and I think, *But why is your church not racially diverse? Why are you not intentionally welcoming nonwhite people to your congregation?*

AT LEAST THE WHITE CHURCH IS THINKING ABOUT DIVERSITY

If you're White, perhaps you're thinking, *Here's another angry Black man who doesn't like White people.* I get it. But remember, my wife is a White girl from Darby, Montana, and half of my family is White. Other than my grandparents, my mom, and my dad, the most influential people in my life have been White. I love all people. And in loving all people, we get a better, richer, clearer reflection of God's beauty. It is in the mosaic of the ethnic diversity created by God that we see his beauty in high definition.

In my experience, White churches are open to the idea of planting ethnically diverse churches and transitioning homogeneous churches into ethnically diverse churches. But I have not found Black churches as open to becoming ethnically diverse. In the *Journal for the Scientific Study of Religion,* Duke University sociology professor Mark Chaves wrote:

We do not want to overstate the significance of this increasing ethnic diversity within American congregations. Eighty-six percent

of American congregations (containing 80 percent of religious
service attendees) remain overwhelmingly white or black or
Hispanic or Asian or whatever. . . .

On the ground, this means there are more white congregations with a smattering of minorities. However, the percent of
mainly black churches with some white people is not increasing.[1]

Second-generation Asian and Latino churches also seem to be
somewhat open to ethnically diverse congregations.[2]

IT'S NOT JUST A BLACK-AND-WHITE THING ANYMORE

I was at a meeting with pastors and seminary leaders about how
the church in America remains segregated despite our culture being
ethnically integrated. In attendance were White pastors, Latino pastors, Black pastors, and Asian pastors, yet the panel was comprised
of only Black and White pastors. As the conversation progressed, I
said, "The issue of ethnic diversity and reconciliation in the church
is no longer just a Black and White issue. It's an Asian, Latino,
White, and Black issue now." The other members on the panel just
stared at me, but the Latino and Asian pastors applauded!

For so long in our country it's just been a Black and White issue,
but that's not the case anymore. Even when I use the term *Asian*,
it encapsulates at least thirty-four ethnicities.[3] Fueled by immigration and birthrates, the population of the church in America is no
longer restricted to two options. God in his sovereignty has brought
"every nation, tribe, and tongue" to America. For the first time in
American history, at the office, the coffee shop, the movie theater,

and the library, you will inevitably interact with someone of a different race or ethnic group than you. By 2060 there will be a less than "one-in-three chance that the next person you meet will share your race or ethnicity, whatever it is: White, Black, Native American, Asian, Native Hawaiian or Hispanic."[4] And on the world stage, by 2050, "72 percent of Christians will live in Africa, Asia, and Latin America, and a sizable share of the remainder will have roots in one or more of those continents."[5]

My heart is burdened with the thought that without a gospel-centered, Jesus-focused missional strategy, local churches will be even more segregated within an increasingly multiethnic America. Just because America is becoming more diverse does not mean our local churches will. We have to be intentional. If we aren't, we will build churches around our own ethnic tribes.

IMPROVING RACE RELATIONS

So here's the question: Why is the Black church seemingly not as open to planting and building ethnically diverse churches? My attempt to answer this question is tempered by the fact that I have never been a member of a Black church. I grew up unchurched, and the first church my wife and I joined was a homogeneous White megachurch. Nevertheless, I believe local Black churches' lack of desire to have ethnically diverse churches is rooted in the tumultuous history of race relations in America. Let's remember that the Civil Rights Act became law in 1964, which is within the lifetime of many Americans. Efrem Smith, CEO and president of World

Impact, a ministry committed to transforming urban communities, gave me three reasons he believes the Black church is not eager to develop multiethnic churches:

1. Because so many issues confront African Americans, there is still a need for a church that exclusively focuses on evangelism, discipleship, and mission in the African American context.
2. Because race and racism continue to be an issue in America, there is a need for a church that equips African Americans to live their faith fruitfully within the reality of racism.
3. Because the Black community still fears that Whites don't know how to join something without operating in privilege and dominating, there is the thought that many Whites will listen to Black pastors but they don't really respect them and they're not willing to submit to one.[6]

I respect Efrem as a leader and a friend, and God has used him to build a thriving multiethnic church. He provides much-needed clarity as we navigate the twenty-first century. In his book *The Post-Black Church and Post-White Church,* he wrote, "A post-black, post-white church unplugs us from the sinful and unbiblical race matrix of black and white and liberates us to love in an otherworldly, countercultural kingdom church and reconciling community."[7]

Efrem pointed out legitimate fears and concerns about race in America, but what better community is there for these fears and concerns to be healed than in the context of multiethnic churches. It is imperative that the Black church, leading with forgiveness, hearts filled with reconciliation, and gospel-centered leadership, move beyond the well-dug trenches of the past to forge a new multiethnic future.

THEOLOGICALLY DRIVEN, NOT SOCIOLOGICALLY DRIVEN

In my experience, some aspects of the White church are open to ethnic diversity, but this has to do more with sociology and paternalism than gospel-centered theology. In conversations over the years with my White pastor friends who want their local churches to become multiethnic, I would ask about their motivation, and they would give me sociological reasons: the demographics are changing, and we really need to help poor people—as if minorities are the only poor people out there. A young, affluent White church member might talk about reaching out to poor minorities but forget about reaching the Wall Street crowd that sank our economy with subprime loans and predatory lending. Wall Street needs Jesus and his transformative power just as much as people in the hood.

Paternalism means to manage or govern the affairs of another like a father would for a child. Often my White pastor friends, or White Christians in general, approached minorities from a posture of "We will save you," "We have the answers," or "Just follow our leadership and you'll be okay." Building gospel-centered, multiethnic churches will have positive sociological implications; however, leaders should desire to build multiethnic local churches for theological and missiological reasons.

Gospel-Shaped Leaders Don't Just See Black and White

It's essential for Black and White pastors to open our eyes to the phenomenal Latino and Asian pastors and leaders in the church in America who are in the vanguard of innovative, Christ-exalting ministry. These brothers and sisters are providing another narrative that deepens and widens our understanding of God's story, and we need to hear their voices. We need to learn from their experiences. Personally, my Asian pastor friends, like Eugene Cho, lead pastor of Quest Community Church in Seattle, Washington, and Ryan Kwon, lead pastor of Resonate Church in Fremont, California, who lead multiethnic churches, and Dr. Soong-Chan Rah, the Milton B. Engebretson Associate Professor of Church Growth and Evangelism at North Park Theological Seminary, and Professor Christopher Yuan at Moody Bible Institute have richly blessed me and helped me grow as a man and pastor. Their unique experiences and cultural backgrounds add to my life and increase the effectiveness of my understanding.

First-Generation and Second-Generation Issues

One of the issues the church will need to compassionately and innovatively address is the first-generation and second-generation issues that develop within immigrant churches. My friend Ryan Kwon addressed the issue in a recent email:

> The difference between first and second generation:
> There will always be a need for 1st generation ministries. As

long as America is a free country, as long as the gospel is an agent that embraces and makes whole those who are considered aliens, the 1st generation churches must thrive. But what about the 2nd generation? Their experience is quite different than the 1st gen experience. Unlike the 1st generation, the 2nd generation is without the significant barriers to fight through, namely, the language and the culture barrier. Our parents came to this country without speaking the language, which limited their social engagement. As a result, they were drawn toward things that are familiar to them, like food and people. The 2nd generation does not have this barrier being born in the States. Our parents simultaneously fought the cultural barrier. Things from the Western milieu didn't make sense to them, while the Westerners didn't understand them. For example, when a Westerner spills the tray in a cafeteria, the crowd looks. A few of them might even offer to help pick up what was spilled. In a high honor culture, when someone spills, they don't look, as to preserve that person's honor and to cover up their shame. This is an example of the cultural difference, and our parent's honor culture was mistaken for passivity. The 2nd generation doesn't struggle with this barrier. Many of them have extracted the benefits of the Eastern culture but have been assimilated to the Western culture. Immigrants need a place to land, to be ministered to, to have the gospel preached to. However the needs of their offspring, the 2nd generation, have altogether different needs.

The 2nd generation's desire for multi/transculturalism:

I am a 2nd generation Korean American and have the penchant for multiethnic, multiclass local churches for three reasons:

First, as mentioned above, I don't feel the limitations as my parents did with their language and cultural barriers. While these limitations naturally build towards ethnocentrality, quite honestly, I feel freed from it.

Second reason why I have a penchant for multiethnic, multiclass local church is because of the "mission." My world is not ethnocentric. My neighbors, co-workers, and my softball team are not all Korean Americans. They are from all different parts of the world, including America. So if God has called me to reach people with the gospel in the neighborhood I live and the park I play in, it lends itself to a multicultural mission, which leads itself to a multiethnic ecclesiology.

Third reason is the gospel. Christ breached all barriers as a sinless God coming to earth to redeem sinful people; as a healthy person to restore the sick; as a rich person to relieve the poor, as a live person to revive the dead.[8]

I agree with Ryan that the first-generation immigrant church will be needed for the reasons stated above. But I would love to see immigrant churches connected to nonimmigrant churches in a meaningful relationship to help with the transition of the second generation and to display reconciliation and unity. This will take intentionality, meaningful dialogue, and creativity. What exactly does that look like? I'm not sure. It's up to you to take the gospel and figure it out. And I also agree with Ryan on the needs of the second generation and the need to plant and build local multiethnic churches.

If we are truly going to be missional, we need the mosaic

of all of God's people. Every tribe and tongue is in a neighborhood near you. It's time for the church to truly be missional if we're going to reach our country that is increasingly ethnically diverse. But mission doesn't start with the church; it started with God.

GOD, THE FIRST MISSIONARY

Long before the apostle Paul went to the Gentiles on his missionary journeys to proclaim the unsearchable riches of Christ, God himself was the first missionary. God, in his eternal counsel and community of three, envisioned a future world where

> [They] sang a new song, saying,
> "Worthy are you to take the scroll
> and to open its seals,
> for you were slain, and by your blood you ransomed
> people for God
> from every tribe and language and people and nation,
> and you have made them a kingdom and priests to
> our God,
> and they shall reign on the earth."
>
> Then I looked, and I heard around the throne and the living creatures and the elders the voice of many angels, numbering myriads of myriads and thousands of thousands, saying with a loud voice,

"Worthy is the Lamb who was slain,

to receive power and wealth and wisdom and might

and honor and glory and blessing!" (Revelation 5:9–12)

God the Father and God the Holy Spirit were pleased to see a multiethnic people adore and praise Jesus. But in order for this future world to be a reality, God himself had to initiate it. This is called grace. God the Father sent the Son to redeem humanity, then the Father and the Son sent the Holy Spirit, and now the Father, the Son, and the Holy Spirit send and empower Jesus' bride, the church, on mission to be ambassadors of reconciliation (see 2 Corinthians 5:18–21). At Transformation Church, we call this being mission-shaped, meaning all that we do is shaped by God's redemptive mission. We say we don't have a missions department, because the church is a missionary movement. Every Christ follower is a missionary, either locally or globally. We are a *glocal* (global and local) church: we reach out to our immediate area and in partnership with international mission opportunities.

Since the early 2000s, the term *missional* has been a buzzword. I'm tired of it because it is not being understood the way the apostle Paul meant it.

THE MEANING OF A MISSIONAL CHURCH

The term *missional church* gained prominence with the 1998 publication of *Missional Church: A Vision for the Sending of the Church in North America,* edited by Darrell L. Guder. Guder's team of authors focused on missiologist Lesslie Newbigin's use of the term *missio Dei* ("mission of God"). The essence of the book is that the church is a sent people, a missionary people. The church exists because it has a mission. Here's a sample of the book's message:

> The church represents the divine reign as its *sign and foretaste*. Themes woven into the fabric of the book of Ephesians illustrate this intended meaning. When the author speaks of the breaking down of the barriers between Jews and Gentiles ([Ephesians] 2:11ff.) that has resulted from expansion of the gospel mission to the Gentile world, he states that this profound social change within the small community of Christians represents God's purposes for the world: "that he might create in himself one new humanity in place of two, thus making peace" (2:15). The emerging multicultural church is here a foretaste of God's redeeming purposes for the world, which is the mystery now revealed: "that is, the Gentiles have become fellow heirs, members of the same body, and sharers in the promise in Christ Jesus through the gospel" (3:6). This point is even more explicit when the church is described as the sign of God's wisdom for the cosmos: "so that through the church the wisdom of God in its rich variety might now be made known to the rulers and authorities in the heavenly places" (3:10). As a sign represents something else and as a foretaste represents something yet to come, the church points away from itself to what God is going to complete.[9]

Despite this biblical exposition of God's heart for the local church on earth, the missional movement in America has missed the most important gospel reality. If the church in America is going to be truly missional and equip local congregations, we must grab hold of Jesus' heart for diverse local churches.

MULTIETHNIC CHURCHES ARE ABOUT THE GREAT COMMANDMENT TO LOVE

As I said in chapter 3, a vision of the future transforms what you do today. At Transformation Church, our vision is that one day thousands and thousands of people, in response to the unsearchable riches of Christ, would love God with all of their hearts, minds, souls, and strength and that they would love their neighbors—White, Black, Asian, Latino, mixed ethnicities, rich, poor, middle class—as they love themselves. Wouldn't that be a beautiful world? That experience would be heaven on earth, and it would be a sign and foretaste of Revelation 5:9–12. It's thoroughly God's heart. This is Jesus' Great Commandment and the Great Commission. When he was questioned about this, Jesus had this response:

> And behold, a lawyer stood up to put him to the test, saying, "Teacher, what shall I do to inherit eternal life?" He said to him, "What is written in the Law? How do you read it?" And he answered, "You shall love the Lord your God with all your heart and with all your soul and with all your strength and with all your mind, and your neighbor as yourself." (Luke 10:25–27)

At the end of every service, we say in unison, "Upward! Inward! Outward!" Upward means to love God completely, because he first loved us. Inward means to love yourself correctly, because Christ lives in us. And outward means to love your neighbor compassionately because of Christ's love through us.

In Luke 10, Jesus shares the Great Commandment, which is the Hebrew *Shema*. Jesus combines Deuteronomy 6:4–5 and Leviticus 18:19 to make the commandment. If there was ever a passage of Scripture that reflected God's heart for reconciliation and the grace-centered construction of multiethnic churches, it's this text. Luke's version of the Great Commandment is the same as Matthew's, but the context of Luke is unique.

Luke was a Gentile, an outsider, and outsiders see things differently than insiders. He introduced a lawyer, or man well versed in the Mosaic Law, who tested Jesus to see if he would distort the *Shema*, which is the first four of the Ten Commandments and focus on loving God. The last six deal with loving your neighbor as yourself. But Jesus affirmed the *Shema*, catching the lawyer. So what did the lawyer do? Luke said, "desiring to justify himself," he asked Jesus, "And who is my neighbor?" Then Jesus went to work:

> A man was going down from Jerusalem to Jericho, and he fell among robbers, who stripped him and beat him and departed, leaving him half dead. Now by chance a priest was going down that road, and when he saw him he passed by on the other side. So likewise a Levite, when he came to the place and saw him, passed by on the other side. (Luke 10:30–32)

In telling this story to a Jewish audience, Jesus fleshed out what it means to love your neighbor. Jesus said a priest, who was supposed to love people, avoided the victim who may have been dead. Then the Levite, who assisted the priest, did the same thing. Then Jesus detonated a gospel bomb:

> But a Samaritan, as he journeyed, came to where he was, and when he saw him, he had compassion. He went to him and bound up his wounds, pouring on oil and wine. Then he set him on his own animal and brought him to an inn and took care of him. And the next day he took out two denarii and gave them to the innkeeper, saying, "Take care of him, and whatever more you spend, I will repay you when I come back." Which of these three, do you think, proved to be a neighbor to the man who fell among the robbers? [The lawyer] said, "The one who showed him mercy." And Jesus said to him, "You go, and do likewise." (Luke 10:33–37)

In a shocking turn of events, Jesus made the despised Samaritan an example of what it means to love one's neighbor. As I noted in chapter 4, Jews and Samaritans hated one another. Here's a little more insight as to why.

> According to 2 Kings, the foreigners resettled in Israel were taught about Yahweh but worshiped Him alongside their native gods. (See 2 Kings 17:28, 33.) This mixing of ethnic and religious marks of Hebrew identity led the Jews to reject Samaritans as half-breed Gentiles. The deep division between Jews and Samaritans dated back to the Jewish return from Babylonian exile in the late sixth century BC when the Jews rejected the Samaritans' request to assist in rebuilding the temple, citing their shared worship of Yahweh.

(See Ezra 4:1–3.) After that rejection, the Samaritans actively opposed the rebuilding of the temple in Jerusalem. (See Ezra 4:4–24.) Their lack of a pure Israelite ancestry contributed to their rejection when Jewish leaders began to emphasize bloodline as a marker of identity and prevented intermarriage with the non-Jews living in Palestine. (See Ezra 9.) The Samaritans used a dialect of Hebrew and preserved a version of the Pentateuch that supported their identification of Mount Gerizim as the holy mountain of God and the site for their sacred worship. The Hasmonean ruler John Hyrcanus further exacerbated Jewish-Samaritan relations by destroying Shechem and leveling the Samaritan temple in 128 BC. Samaritans rejected the Jerusalem temple as illegitimate and had their own priesthood. They also expected a messianic figure based on Deuteronomy 18:18, in which God promised Moses that He would "raise up for them a prophet like you," referring to Moses. Jews and Samaritans had a mutual antipathy based on ethnic, religious, and political barriers.[10]

In addition, according to the Jewish historian Josephus, while Coponius was procurator in AD 6, some Samaritans secretly joined some Jewish Passover pilgrims and entered the temple. Once inside the temple, they desecrated it by spreading human bones in the porticoes and in the sanctuary. The Jews saw this as the worst desecration possible! Then, in AD 51, people from the Samaritan village of Ginae murdered some Jewish pilgrims on their way to Jerusalem.[11] Although the Ginae tragedy occurred after Jesus told the good Samaritan story, it demonstrates how much Jews and Samaritans despised each other.

Jesus, however, said that loving your neighbor involves loving those you are supposed to hate, and you love them by doing what the Samaritan did for the Jewish victim on the road to Jericho. To love someone means to assume their pain, to embrace their story, to invite them into your family so much that it costs you something, even though there is hostility. Only love can defeat hate. Multiethnic local churches have the power to teach us to love by placing us in relationship with others who we do not know.

It is not by accident that Luke, the author of Acts, recorded that Jesus told the disciples to go to Jerusalem, Judea, Samaria, and the ends of the earth in Acts 1:8. Luke pointed out that it was only because of persecution that the Jewish believers went to Samaria: "Philip went down to the city of Samaria and proclaimed to them the Christ" (Acts 8:5).

Can you imagine how the Samaritans must have viewed this enemy preaching love to them? Can you imagine traditionally homogeneous churches creating intentionally inclusive ministry environments and preaching Christ in order to be ambassadors of love, reconciliation, and transformation? I long for that day. I pray the Lord lets me see it.

May we have churches that reflect Jesus' heart and Philip's example of preaching Christ to the Samaritans among us? The world needs good news from the community that is supposed to embody and herald the good news of the gospel! This is what it means to be missional: we are on a mission, sent by the Father, Son, and Holy Spirit to be people who share the good news in a world filled with bad news. And we are not to be selective with whom we share the good news. If our churches are in ethnically diverse areas, then we are to share and build communities that are inclusive so we can reach all people.

GOOD NEWS CHURCHES

When we were in the beginning stages of planting Transformation Church in 2009, pastors asked me, "Who is your target group?" I answered, "Sinners—Asian ones, Latino ones, White ones, Black ones, and mixed ethnicity ones," and they looked at me like I was a Martian. Too many pastors in America are influenced by the homogeneous unit principle and, therefore, are taught to target a certain ethnic group within a certain socioeconomic status. The gospel of Christ would not allow me not to try to reach *all* people in our missional context, because all people are in need of the good news, and we need good-news local churches to get that message out.

What is the good news? It's the announcement that Israel's King and Messiah has accomplished what he came to do. Jesus has defeated sin, death, and evil through his sinless life, his substitutionary, atoning death on the cross, his resurrection, and his ascension to the right hand of his Father, where he is now our High Priest, making intercession on our behalf.

By grace alone, through the Holy Spirit's power, people who trust in Jesus are redeemed and swept up into his glorious kingdom. This redeemed multicolored people become a "chosen race, a royal priesthood, a holy nation," proclaiming the "excellencies of him who called [them] out of darkness into his marvelous light" (1 Peter 2:9–10).

EVANGELISM MUST BE ROOTED IN A GOSPEL-CENTERED VISION

Ninety-four percent of local churches in America are not growing.[12]

Let that sink in.

This breaks my heart, and it should break yours. This statistic means that more and more people in America don't know the redemptive power of Jesus Christ. This fact will increase divorce, addiction, injustice, greed, sexual immorality, idolatry, oppression, and a multitude of other sins that destroy people's lives. We need evangelistic local churches fueled by Christ followers who see themselves as missionaries. We need good-news local churches filled with good-news people.

EVANGELISM MUST BE ROOTED IN GOSPEL-CENTERED WORSHIP

Gospel-centered worship is not simply singing but a lifestyle submerged in, interwoven with, and united to Jesus' very life. When worship is a lifestyle, evangelism is not an activity but an identity. By God's grace, in five short years, Transformation Church has baptized over fifteen hundred people and seen over three thousand come to faith. Our congregation is a passionate, Spirit-enabled, missionary/evangelist community. Compelled by the love of Christ, we are fishers of men.

An example of this evangelistic/missionary passion fueled by the love of Christ are the Vinroots, a White couple in their early seventies. Robert and Pat Vinroot exhibit this love for the others, not out of paternalism, but because they are rooted in Christ's love. Pat was in a bookstore when she found my first book, *Hero*, on the shelves. After reading the book, she found out that I was in Charlotte, not too many miles from a prison where she and her husband had been volunteering. As she read my book, she said she sensed God telling her to call me. She invited me to speak at Kershaw Correctional Institution near Lancaster, South Carolina.

After preaching, the inmates asked if they could receive copies of sermons to watch on a weekly basis. Soon after this meeting, we launched Transformation Church Kershaw Prison. Through Kershaw Prison chaplain Gerry Potoka and Transformation Church outreach director Ken Lake, we now have ten inmate-led small groups, a process for leadership development, and over a hundred men have been baptized in a year.

As Transformation Church and I have grown in our relationship with the men of Kershaw, they tell me the reason they want to be part of Transformation Church is that they felt we treated them as people and equals, not projects and subservient people. They said we made them feel valued, loved, and empowered. People in need do not require paternalism; they need someone to treat them as equals and to believe in them.

Evangelism Must Be Rooted in Gospel-Centered Discipleship

Discipleship isn't just knowing more about Jesus; it's about knowing Jesus personally and being transformed into his image through constant exposure of the gospel of grace in the context of a local church. Jesus' life and mission becomes ours as we live by faith in him in the everydayness of life by the Spirit's power as his church. The deeper a person's discipleship, the deeper they go into the culture to reach lost people.

We firmly believe that the growth in conversions we have experienced is directly connected to our Spirit-empowered effectiveness in making disciples. A disciple becomes like the teacher, and our Teacher is Jesus who came "to seek and save the lost" (Luke 19:10). Our Teacher said, "Follow me, and I will make you fishers of men" (Matthew 4:19). We believe that spiritually mature people love Jesus and want lost people to love him too.

EVANGELISM MUST BE ROOTED IN GOSPEL-CENTERED SERVING

One of the things we often say is, "If our community doesn't change, then we shouldn't be here." One of the most effective ways we have found for impacting our community is through serving our public schools. In four years, we have adopted four public schools.

We serve them by having teacher appreciation lunches, mentoring students, offering grief counseling, funding leadership programs with financial resources and people, and feeding more than 125 families per weekend through a backpack meal ministry. By serving our schools, we've seen students, administrators, parents, and teachers come to faith in Christ and serve at Transformation Church.

Recently, Indian Land Middle School was one of forty-four middle schools in America to win the prestigious State School of Character award. Principal Chris Thorpe said "he was amazed and that Transformation Church was truly the hands and feet of Jesus" and that he was thankful for our partnership.

What if every Jesus-centered, gospel-of-grace-loving local

church in America adopted the public schools? The results would be epic.

EVANGELISM MUST BE ROOTED IN GOSPEL-CENTERED LIVING

We don't have an evangelism training class. When the woman at the well in John 4:4–42 encountered Jesus, she immediately ran back to her city and shared about her experience with Jesus. We call that a grace story. We want our people to simply share their grace stories as the Holy Spirit provides opportunities to do so. We equip our people to intercede, invest, and invite. We teach our people that before they talk to someone about Jesus, they should talk to Jesus about that someone. We teach them to simply love people, share their grace story, and add value to the lives of those they encounter, regardless of their response. We teach our people apologetics through our sermons and small groups. We also teach them to invite the lost people in their spheres of influence to a weekend service. I firmly believe that the same gospel that justifies the sinner is the same gospel that sanctifies and glorifies the saint.

Lost people need Jesus. Saved people need Jesus. We never outgrow the gospel; we grow deeper into the gospel. Pastors ask, "Is your church seeker sensitive?" I answer, "We are Jesus sensitive." When glorious, beautiful King Jesus is lifted up, he will draw all men to himself (see John 12:32). Jesus finds the lost and builds believers. We also believe that reaching the lost must go beyond weekend worship experiences. Church is more than a weekend event. Church is a community of people living out the Great Commandment and the Great Commission as missionaries who have been transformed by Jesus.

EVANGELISM MUST BE ROOTED IN GOSPEL-CENTERED RELIANCE ON THE HOLY SPIRIT

Transformation Church has never had enough money to accomplish the vision God has laid before us. Our lack of resources taught us to rely on the infinite resources of God the Holy Spirit. Pastor, your financial lack may be the very advantage that takes the church you serve to greater effectiveness. We've found the bigger the risk we take to reach lost people, the more lost people come to faith through the ministry of our church and the more financial resources God provides to get it done.

Our mission and evangelism extend to Brazil, China, Haiti, India, Rwanda, and Sudan. As we develop relationships with our brothers and sisters overseas, we grow and are blessed too. After my daughter and I went to Kolkata, India, my life was forever transformed by what I experienced. The believers there inspired me by their selfless, sacrificial, Jesus-centered lives.

Evangelism in the twenty-first century is the same as it was in the first century: saved people longing to see unsaved people come to know Jesus.

In the next chapter, we are going to open up a treasure chest that the apostle Paul called the "unsearchable riches of Christ" (Ephesians 3:8). Let's see the gospel in high definition.

STUDY QUESTIONS, REFLECTIONS, AND PRAYER

1. Examine sociology professor Mark Chaves's statement:

   Still, in an upcoming issue of the *Journal for the Scientific Study of Religion*, Chaves wrote: We do not want to overstate the significance of this increasing ethnic diversity within American congregations. Eighty-six percent of American congregations (containing 80 percent of religious service attendees) remain overwhelmingly white or black or Hispanic or Asian or whatever. . . .

   Chaves said in an interview, "On the ground, this means there are more white congregations with a smattering of minorities. However, the percent of mainly black churches with some white people is not increasing."[13]

2. *"Gospel-shaped leaders are burdened with the thought that without a gospel-centered, Jesus-focused, missional strategy, local churches will be even more segregated within an increasingly multiethnic America."* In what ways do you see this in your community or denomination?

3. Can you relate to the need to being willing to listen to the narratives of people who are different from you? Think about the difference between partnership and mutual learning versus paternalism and spiritual colonialism.

4. What do you think is the most effective way for you to handle the complexities and difficulties of reaching first- and second-generation Americans with the gospel?
5. Do you have a strategy of evangelism? Discuss the following ideas about evangelism:
   a. Evangelism must be rooted in gospel-centered vision.
   b. Evangelism must be rooted in gospel-centered worship.
   c. Evangelism must be rooted in gospel-centered discipleship.
   d. Evangelism must be rooted in gospel-centered serving.
   e. Evangelism must be rooted in gospel-centered reliance on the Holy Spirit.

PRAYER

Father, Son, and Spirit, you are the first missionary. And now, by grace, you send us, your church, missionally to our diverse spheres of influence. Lord, bless us to reach the lost and disciple them so they, too, can be sent on mission for your glory, their joy, and for the sake of the world. In Jesus' name, amen.

SIX

SEEING THE BEAUTIFUL
GOSPEL STORY

Blessed be the God and Father of our Lord Jesus
Christ, who has blessed us in Christ with every
spiritual blessing in the heavenly places.
—EPHESIANS 1:3

PEOPLE ARE HURTING

People are hurting deeply, even to the point of great despair. Despite our technological advances and financial resources, we don't have the capability to heal all of our hurting. Only King Jesus—the One who was dealt the worst hurt of all—can heal us. It is only by his wounds and scars that ours are healed.

The day I began writing this chapter, I received the following email that powerfully illustrates this:

> A couple months ago my mom heard you on the radio and asked me if I would go one Sunday to Transformation Church with her. I stopped going to church about six years ago when I moved out because my dad couldn't make me go any more. So I decided to go to Transformation Church with my mom because she needed it. My mom suffered from bad depression and was a bad [alcoholic]. This put her in some bad places for months at a time. It destroyed our family.
>
> So we went to Transformation Church and you were preaching through a sermon series called "Out of Control." God really turned my mom around! These last few months my mom was a different person. We would talk about your sermons throughout the week. I want to thank you because my mom recently died in a car accident. I know you're just the messenger, but if you weren't doing what you are doing I don't know if my mom would be in such a good place before she died. And it got me back in church. I look forward to attending Transformation Church on Sundays now. I shook your hand this morning after the first service and told you, "Thank you." You just don't know how [deep] that thank you was. I know where my mom is.
>
> Thank you.

My heart is both joyful and saddened by reading this email. People are hurting and they need the gospel. But what is the gospel?

WHAT IS THE GOSPEL?

How we answer the question "What is the gospel?" will determine the disciples we make and the churches we build. It will determine the effectiveness of local churches in a world of darkness. Will local churches be a city on a hill lit up by the presence and power of Jesus? I propose that the gospel is bigger, richer, and more beautiful than we realize. The gospel is about a King, a kingdom, and a people who are indwelt, empowered, and gifted to do the King's bidding here and now as they march toward the new heaven and the new earth.[1]

In the West, especially in America, we tend to think individualistically about the gospel. Sadly, we often turn the King of kings into a divine butler who exists to answer our self-centered prayer requests. Instead of the church orbiting around Jesus and his redemptive purposes, we want him to orbit around us and help us achieve the American dream.

FIRST IMPORTANCE

The apostle Paul said, "For I delivered to you as of first importance what I also received: that Christ died for our sins in accordance with the Scriptures, that he was buried, that he was raised on the third day in accordance with the Scriptures, and that he appeared to Cephas, then to the twelve" (1 Corinthians 15:3–5).

The word *gospel* isn't even a Christian word. Christians actually took the word from the Romans. In the first century, the word *gospel* was used to describe the good news that a new emperor had been enthroned. Messengers, or heralds, would be sent out to announce this information throughout the empire.

A herald's message was something like this: "We have good

news to announce! There is a new emperor. His name is Tiberius Caesar. Bow your knee to him." The new emperor was called "Lord" and "Savior" and expected to bless the world by bringing peace, prosperity, and justice. Also, the emperor was called *pontifex maximus*, which means "chief priest." In accordance with the emperor cult, the Romans believed that when an emperor ascended to heaven at his death, he was enthroned as a divine being; therefore, he was called "son of god."[2]

For the first-century followers of the Jewish Messiah in this culture, this belief was false. They said, "We have the real gospel. There is a true King, who is Lord of the universe and Savior of humanity. His name is Jesus, the Prince of Peace, the true and great High Priest. The true King is the eternal Son of God who will bless the world by bringing salvation, peace, prosperity, and justice through his life, death, resurrection, and ascension. Every knee will bow and every tongue will confess that he is Lord."

So the apostles, or "sent ones," pursued this mission across the Roman Empire, heralding this gospel. As Jews and Gentiles believed this gospel and came to faith in Jesus, multiethnic congregations of the true King were established through the empire as a sign and foretaste that the kingdom of God had invaded earth. The apostle Paul, a Jew steeped in the story of Israel, knew that Jesus was Israel's Messiah, the one true King and Lord of the universe who invaded the earth with his kingdom, and who now, by grace, offers salvation to the Jews and Gentiles.

These ethnically diverse people, by faith in the finished work of Jesus, became God's multiethnic, multiclass people, who, according to the apostle Peter, were "a chosen race, a royal priesthood, a holy nation, a people for his own possession" who would join Jesus as "sent ones," invading the earth with the kingdom of God's marvelous light (see 1 Peter 2:9–10).

This gospel story is bigger, richer, and more beautiful than just me and my salvation. The gospel is astronomically rich, so rich that Paul said the gospel provides us with every spiritual blessing in Christ.

THE MULTIETHNIC LOCAL CHURCHES OF EPHESUS

Every one of Paul's letters addressed how the gospel forms Jewish-Gentile multiethnic local churches that function as a sign and foretaste of Jesus' rule and reign. In the first-century Greco-Roman world, multiethnic local churches were not a style of church but the only expression of local churches outside of Jerusalem. The New Testament says nothing of building or planting homogeneous local churches.

We are now going to explore the spiritual blessings we have in Christ by looking at the first two chapters of Ephesians. This is not an exhaustive commentary, but I want to point out some overlooked aspects of what Paul said in these passages about what the gospel accomplishes: the creation of multiethnic local churches.

Ephesus was a booming, ethnically diverse port city in Asia Minor (modern Turkey). It was also the capital of the province of Asia. Ephesus would be comparable to any large city in America. As we learn in Acts 19, Paul went to Ephesus on his second missionary journey and spent three years there establishing congregations.

While Paul was imprisoned around AD 60, he wrote a beautiful letter to the young congregations that he had planted in Ephesus. The apostle wanted them to see that their unity and reconciliation in Christ was bigger than just them and that it pointed to a greater reality: God's redemptive purposes. Ephesians 2:19–22 expresses this gospel reality:

> So then you are no longer strangers and aliens, but you are fellow citizens with the saints and members of the household of God, built on the foundation of the apostles and prophets, Christ Jesus himself being the cornerstone, in whom the whole structure, being joined together, grows into a holy temple in the Lord. In him you also are being built together into a dwelling place for God by the Spirit.

Let's peer into the treasure chest called "every spiritual blessing in the heavenly places" (Ephesians 1:3).

Paul begins this letter with one long sentence in the original Greek, praising God for blessing his people through the completed work of Christ. For three chapters the apostle reminds and teaches the churches at Ephesus that God, by the Spirit's power, has given them every spiritual blessing in Christ so they could be empowered to be a sign and foretaste of the new heaven and new earth. The diverse congregations scattered throughout Ephesus were a microcosm of God's overarching plan for humanity. God in Christ, through the Holy Spirit, had supplied all the Ephesian churches would need to live as a reconciled, unified family. God gave them every spiritual blessing for a greater purpose than just their individual salvation.

He gave them grace to show the world his purpose for all of humanity: reconciliation.

WE ARE SAINTS (EPHESIANS 1:1–2)

Paul began by stating that he is a "sent one," an apostle of Jesus. He then addressed the letter to the "saints" at Ephesus who are faithful in Christ Jesus. Despite his hearing that the Jews and Gentiles were not displaying unity or reconciliation, he addressed these issues in chapters 4 and 5 and calls these Christ followers "saints." A saint is "a holy one who is set apart for God's purposes." Despite their unholy actions toward each other, Paul declared them to be saints because of the actions of Jesus. The very holiness of Jesus is imparted to God's people as a gift. In an act of heart-exploding grace, God's people become as holy as Jesus, not based on the lives they live, but based on the perfect life that Jesus lived.

WE ARE BLESSED (EPHESIANS 1:3)

Paul made a spectacular declaration by writing that the church at Ephesus had "every spiritual blessing in the heavenly places." The key that unlocks the treasure chest and gives us access to the unsearchable riches of Christ is Jesus himself. That is, Jesus is the treasure. Through faith in him, as the Holy Spirit prepares our hearts, we are supernaturally united to Jesus. Theologians call this "union life" in Christ. Our union life in Christ is the sum total of what salvation is. To be united with Jesus means that all of who Jesus is and all of what Jesus accomplished is attributed to us as a gift of grace. Jesus doesn't merely change our lives; Jesus exchanges our dead life for his eternal life. To be "in Christ" means that we have been incorporated into him and he into us. The gospel reality of our union life in Christ is so important that the apostles Paul and John use the phrase "in Christ" 38 times, "in Christ Jesus" 51 times, "in him" 21 times, "in the Lord" 44 times, and other similar phrases no less than 216 times.[3]

Sadly, preachers, teachers, and Christians in general often gloss over our being *in* Christ. We can't be and do what God calls us to if we fail to realize what Jesus has done and what he will do through us. Because we are in Christ, God the Father looks at Jesus as our representative, and his sinless life, atoning death on the cross, resurrection, and ascension are considered by God the Father to be *our* accomplishments as well. Then practically or experientially, as we live by faith in Jesus and his completed work, we undergo the transforming benefits of our union life with Jesus as the Holy Spirit indwells and empowers us.

WE ARE CHOSEN (EPHESIANS 1:4)

According to Paul, God the Father chose us in Christ before the foundation of the world. Paul communicates to the Jew and Gentile congregations of Ephesus that before the world even began, they had been *chosen* in Christ. Just as Israel was chosen by God to be light to those in darkness (see Deuteronomy 7:6), now the church is God's chosen instrument to be that light.

From the eternal perspective, they were—just as we are—elected or chosen in Christ.[4] In an act of immeasurable grace, God moved *because* He is love (see 1 John 4:8, 16) and chose his own eternal Son to be humanity's Savior and representative; therefore, *whosoever* believes in him finds his election in him. It is only through God the

Holy Spirit preparing the hearts of humanity that we can receive or reject God's generous offer. Without God the Holy Spirit convicting our hearts and drawing us near, we are hopeless.

As a result of our election, we are, by faith, united with him and now possess every spiritual blessing in him, empowering us to live on earth in unified communities, as reconciled people, to praise God's glorious grace.[5]

We Are Holy and Blameless (Ephesians 1:4)

Paul said the church at Ephesus is "holy and blameless before him" (Ephesians 1:4). As I discussed earlier in this chapter, the holiness of Jesus is ours too. We did nothing to earn it. Jesus did everything and earned it for us. We are set apart for God's purpose, which is to create a new multiethnic family that acts as God's temple on earth and reflects God's glory, according to Paul (Ephesians 2:19–22).

Because we are also blameless, God the Father sees no sins or faults in us, because Jesus took our sins and faults upon himself on the cross. And in the resurrection, the church that is united with Jesus is clothed in Jesus' blamelessness as a gift. Therefore the Jews and Gentiles of Ephesus could forgive each other their faults and live in harmony, because Jesus forgave them and declared them blameless.

We Are Loved (Ephesians 1:4–5)

Love is not something God does. Love is who he is in his essential being. God loves and desires the whole of humanity to know his love and become a part of his people. For the church at Ephesus and for us today, it is imperative that we know that God the Father loves us with the same infinite passion that he loves his Son, because we are united with Jesus. It is this love that flows from the eternal heart of God that builds multiethnic local churches. The apostle John said, "If anyone says, 'I love God,' and hates his brother, he is a liar; for he who does not love his brother whom he has seen cannot love God whom he has not seen. And this commandment we have from him: whoever loves God must also love his brother" (1 John 4:20–21).

WE ARE ADOPTED SONS AND DAUGHTERS
(EPHESIANS 1:5)

Next, Paul says that God the Father "predestined us for adoption as sons through Jesus Christ, according to the purpose of his will." Before time began, in the eternal now of God's own being, he determined that whoever believes in his Son would be adopted into his family. In the Greco-Roman world, when a child was adopted, they entered the new family in a privileged position. As adopted children through Jesus, we are privileged children, inheriting every spiritual blessing in Christ. Adoption also must be seen from its Jewish understanding against the background of Israel's relationship with the Lord as his "firstborn son" (see Exodus 4:22; Isaiah 1:2). This relationship was established during the Exodus, when God said: "When Israel was a child, I loved him, and out of Egypt I called my son" (Hosea 11:1).

Because Jews and Gentiles are adopted children of God the Father, they entered a new multiethnic family. Old allegiances and prejudices died, and alliances with their new family were formed.

WE ARE A PEOPLE OF PRAISE (EPHESIANS 1:6)

God gives us this precious gift of adoption "to the praise of his glorious grace, with which he has blessed us in the Beloved." The church at Ephesus was stunned at God's grace so much so that they praised him for his glorious grace. We are to praise God with our words but also by living in unity and reconciliation as God's new multiethnic people; this is the ultimate praise of God's grace. In the ancient world, for unity and reconciliation between Jews and Gentiles to take place, it could only happen by God's grace. It's worthy of praise! Only God's grace could transform hard, hate-filled hearts.

WE ARE REDEEMED (EPHESIANS 1:7)

In addition to these gifts, "In him we have redemption through his blood." This gospel reality means that slaves have been set free from captivity. Just as Israel was enslaved in Egypt, the Jewish and Gentile believers in Ephesus were enslaved to sin, death, and evil, and Jesus has set them free by his blood. The blood of Jesus is powerful. I have to think that when Paul wrote these words, he was thinking that the blood of Jesus set Jews and Gentiles free from ethnocentrism, prejudice, classism, and racism.

WE ARE FORGIVEN (EPHESIANS 1:7–10)

The church at Ephesus was forgiven of "trespasses, according to the riches of his grace, which he lavished upon us, in all wisdom and insight making known to us the mystery of his will, according to his purpose, which he set forth in Christ as a plan for the fullness of time, to unite all things in him, things in heaven and things on earth" (Ephesians 1:7–10).

God's grace is so rich that the church at Ephesus, just like us today, had its past, present, and future sins forgiven by Jesus. The Lamb of God, who was slain before the foundation of the world, forgave us before we were ever born (see Revelation 13:8). The blood of Jesus is a perpetual shower of forgiveness that we stand under. I imagine that Paul reflected on the ancient psalm: "As far as the east is from the west, so far does he remove our transgressions from us" (Psalm 103:12). This forgiveness allowed Jews and Gentiles to forgive each other their past prejudices, conflicts, and hurts. And it can do the same for us today.

The mystery of God's will is that Jews and Gentiles would now form the new people of God and be members of the same body, sharing equally the promise of Christ Jesus (see Ephesians 3:6). This same Jesus can do this in his church today if we are courageous enough to let him.

WE HAVE AN INHERITANCE (EPHESIANS 1:11–12)

Paul continued, "In him we have obtained an inheritance, having been predestined according to the purpose of him who works all things according to the counsel of his will, so that we who were the first to hope in Christ might be to the praise of his glory" (Ephesians 1:11–12).

The "we" in this verse refers to the Jews. In Christ, the Jews, due to their "in Christness" have obtained an inheritance. And God in his sovereignty decided in eternity that all believers would have an inheritance. Paul, in his letter to the Roman churches, described our inheritance in this way: "And if children, then heirs—heirs of God and fellow heirs with Christ, provided we suffer with him in order that we may also be glorified with him" (Romans 8:17).

WE ARE SEALED AND FILLED WITH GOD THE HOLY SPIRIT (EPHESIANS 1:13–14; 5:18)

Paul then turned his words to the Gentiles and said, "In him you also, when you heard the word of truth, the gospel of your salvation, and believed in him, were sealed with the promised Holy Spirit, who is the guarantee of our inheritance until we acquire possession of it, to the praise of his glory" (Ephesians 1:13–14).

In Christ, the Gentiles who heard the gospel and believed were sealed with the promise of the Holy Spirit guaranteeing that Jews and Gentiles would acquire their inheritance to the praise of God's glory. God the Spirit not only eternally seals and keeps the Jews and Gentiles in Christ, but the Spirit also provides the fruit of the Spirit and blesses them with the gifts of the Spirit for the encouragement of the body of Christ and service in the world (see Ephesians 5:18; Galatians 5:22–24).

WE ARE POWERFUL IN CHRIST (EPHESIANS 1:15–22)

Paul wrote that he had heard how the multiethnic churches of Ephesus loved Jesus and each other and that he prayed for them to have more insight into Jesus and knowledge of Jesus. Then he said, "And what is the immeasurable greatness of his power toward us who believe, according to the working of his great might that he worked in Christ when he raised him from the dead and seated him at his right hand in the heavenly places?" (Ephesians 1:19–20).

Paul told the Jews and Gentiles that he had immeasurable power in Christ—the same power of God that had raised Jesus from the dead. It is the power that forged and formed local churches in Ephesus. It is only God's immeasurable power that made enemies brothers and sisters. And Jesus' power can do this today.

All this power and grace are so Jesus could fill the Jews and Gentiles with his very life, thus forming his church and displaying his rule and reign. Our unity and reconciliation is a witness to Jesus' victory.

WE ARE ALIVE (EPHESIANS 2:1–5)

Paul then told the Gentiles they had been spiritually dead in their sins, hell-bound, under God's wrath, but God, who is rich in mercy and great love, made us alive together with the Messiah by grace. God poured out grace after grace on the Gentiles by imparting the life of the resurrected Jesus into them. Jesus' spiritual DNA pulsated through the Gentiles. The same Jesus who walked out of the tomb, now walked out his very life in the Gentiles then—and now. How could we not be unified and reconciled if we are alive with the God who reconciles and unifies?

WE ARE TROPHIES OF GRACE SEATED IN HEAVEN (EPHESIANS 2:6–7)

Because we are in Christ, we are seated with him on his throne at the right hand of the Father. The eternal God of heaven now expresses his heavenly life through us on earth. And God does this so that, for all eternity, he can point to his multiethnic people as trophies of grace. The grace that God gives us in Christ is the same grace that unified and reconciled the Jews and Gentiles of the churches of Ephesus, and it's the same grace that can create multiethnic churches in America and the world today.

We Are Graced (Ephesians 2:8–9)

Paul then wrote: "For by grace you have been saved through faith. And this is not your own doing; it is the gift of God, not a result of works, so that no one may boast" (Ephesians 2:9–10).

In breathtaking fashion, Paul said it is by grace that God has saved us. Grace means that Jesus, from beginning to end, has accomplished everything to save us and bring us into God's family. The sheer weight of what Jesus accomplished can't be earned through our performance or right living; it can only be obtained by faith in the performance of Jesus and perfect, sinless living.

Jesus fulfilled the Law perfectly. Jesus forgave our sins. Jesus rose from the dead, giving us his life. Jesus gave us a gift of unimaginable worth. No one can boast. We are left only boasting in Jesus.

But God didn't do this solely for individual needs. God has done something bigger, richer, and more beautiful than individual salvation.

We Are God's Workmanship (Ephesians 2:10)

But why *did* Jesus give us this grace? "For we are his workmanship, created in Christ Jesus for good works, which God prepared beforehand, that we should walk in them" (Ephesians 2:10). In Christ, Jews and Gentiles and the multiethnic churches in Ephesus are God's workmanship created to do good work that he prepared beforehand that we should walk in them. As mentioned earlier in the book, these good works are the fulfillment of God's covenant with Abraham. The creation of local multiethnic churches is God's covenant fulfillment. God saves us by grace to create diverse local churches where people treat each other with grace, forming a community that is an alternative to an ungracious world.

How do we know this to be true?

WE ARE BROUGHT NEAR TO CHRIST (EPHESIANS 2:11–13)

Paul immediately followed this thought with an admonition: "Therefore remember that at one time you Gentiles in the flesh, called 'the uncircumcision' by what is called the circumcision, which is made in the flesh by hands—remember that you were at that time separated from Christ, alienated from the commonwealth of Israel and strangers to the covenants of promise, having no hope and without God in the world. But now in Christ Jesus you who once were far off have been brought near by the blood of Christ" (Ephesians 2:11–13).

Let's do some review. In Paul's exploration of why God gives us grace, he talked about how Gentiles were once far away, separated from Israel, and strangers to the covenants of promise. The covenant of promise is the covenant God made with Abraham, and Paul said in Galatians: "And the Scripture, foreseeing that God would justify the Gentiles by faith, preached the gospel beforehand to Abraham, saying, 'In you shall all the nations be blessed.' So then, those who are of faith are blessed along with Abraham, the man of faith" (Galatians 3:8–9).

God gives us grace through Jesus so that God displays his faithfulness to Abraham, that Abraham would one day be the father of a big, beautiful multiethnic family. The multiethnic churches at Ephesus in the first century and around the world in the twenty-first century are a foretaste to God's eternal church and restoration and reconciliation of the world. The blood of Jesus doesn't just remove our individual sins; his gracious blood is so powerful it brings Jews and Gentiles near to Christ and one another to form a united community of brothers and sisters.

WE ARE A NEW HUMANITY (EPHESIANS 2:14–16)

Paul went on to say that Jesus, through epic feats of grace, brought peace between Jews and Gentiles and that Jesus broke down the barriers that divided Jews and Gentiles in the temple and the barriers of race and class and gender (see Galatians 3:24–29). As a result of Jesus' work, a new ethnic group is created, made up of Jews and Gentiles. Paul said it this way: "And might reconcile us both to God in one body through the cross, thereby killing the hostility. And he came and preached peace to you who were far off and peace to those who were near" (Ephesians 2:16–17). Jesus preached to those who were far off (Gentiles) and those who were near (Jews).

Homogeneous local churches were foreign to the New Testament because of the gospel that was preached. As a result of the gospel, multiethnic local churches were forged and formed from grace, by grace, and through grace.

We Are Citizens and Members of God's Household (Ephesians 2:18–20)

Paul said that Jews and Gentiles were now fellow citizens and members of God's household. This was revolutionary in the segregated first-century world. These are words that were used to describe Israel, but now Paul used them to describe Jews *and* Gentiles, pointing back again to God's covenant with Abraham. It's as if Paul were saying, "You can do this. You can be the future, eternal church in the present, because you are fellow citizens and members of God's household alive with the presence and power of Jesus." And we can do this today because the same Jesus and same grace are available to us.

We Are God's New Temple (Ephesians 2:20–22)

Paul finished with a flurry of grace: "Built on the foundation of the apostles and prophets, Christ Jesus himself being the cornerstone, in whom the whole structure, being joined together, grows into a holy temple in the Lord. In him you also are being built together into a dwelling place for God by the Spirit" (Ephesians 2:20–22).

It's as if Paul caught his breath and said, "God in Christ by the Spirit has given you Jews and Gentiles grace because you are God's dwelling place and his temple. Heaven and earth now meet in you." God no longer resides in temples made of brick but in multiethnic people who are temples made through the blood of Jesus. And God's glory is seen in high definition because each Jew and Gentile (African, Greek, barbarian, Roman, Asian) was a different-colored brick, a beautiful mosaic.

N. T. Wright observed,

> The larger reality to which this points, the new creation itself, is to be symbolized by the whole church, united and holy. The new temple is to be a place where all the nations will come to worship the God of Abraham, Isaac and Jacob. . . . The reconciliation of Jews and Greeks, particularly was obviously near the heart of Paul's aim. . . . Paul wanted to see as a result of all his labours cross-culturally united worship.[6]

At the heart of the book of Ephesians and all of Paul's letters is that the gospel of Jesus Christ formed multiethnic local churches as a display of God's faithfulness to the covenant he made with Abraham. In America, we have allowed individualism, consumerism, classism, our racist history, and the homogeneous unit principle to hijack the gospel of Jesus Christ.

It's time we begin to see the church in high definition.

STUDY QUESTIONS, REFLECTIONS, AND PRAYER

1. How do you define the gospel? What new definitions do you have after reading this chapter?
2. What are the implications of the following statement: *"Gospel-shaped leaders are committed to God's bigger, richer, and more beautiful story called the gospel."*

3. What steps can you take to increase this understanding of the gospel in your daily life and ministry?

4. Much of this chapter was about understanding Ephesians 1:3–2:22. What did you learn? How does this change how you communicate the gospel?

5. *"Leaders captivated by the gospel refuse to allow individualism, consumerism, classism, our racist history in America, and the homogeneous unit principle to hijack the gospel of Jesus Christ."* How have you seen these ideas affect your church and the church in America?

PRAYER

Father, teach us the unsearchable riches of Christ that we may experience them personally and in a life-giving, transformative way. In Jesus' name, amen.

SEVEN

SEEING THE CHURCH
THROUGH A GOSPEL VISION

*So that through the church the manifold wisdom of
God might now be made known to the rulers and
authorities in the heavenly places. This was according
to the eternal purpose that he has realized in Christ
Jesus our Lord, in whom we have boldness and
access with confidence through our faith in him.*
—EPHESIANS 3:10–12

I HAVE A DREAM

On August 28, 1963, from the steps of the Lincoln Memorial, Dr. Martin Luther King Jr. delivered his world-famous "I Have a Dream" sermon. King's speech moved America toward reconciliation, forgiveness, and hope.

But long before Dr. King uttered a word, even before time ever began, the King of kings had a dream for humanity. The apostle Paul described the King of king's dream when he penned these words:

> So that through the church the manifold wisdom of God might now be made known to the rulers and authorities in the heavenly places. This was according to the eternal purpose that he has realized in Christ Jesus our Lord, in whom we have boldness and access with confidence through our faith in him. (Ephesians 3:10–12)

Paul stated that the King of kings has an "eternal purpose" that was realized in Christ Jesus our Lord. What is this eternal purpose that is so important that it was realized in Christ himself?

Just as God is eternal, our triune King has had an eternal ambition that could be realized by no other than Christ Jesus. God's eternal purpose is Jesus' multiethnic church. The King of kings has eternally thought about forming a people made up of Jews and Gentiles that would be the crown jewel of his possession, the passion of his heart, the love of his life, the embodiment of his kingdom on earth. God's multiethnic church matters to him. And it must matter to us if we are to be faithful to the gospel in our generation.

PLANTING MULTIETHNIC CHURCHES MATTERED TO PAUL

It is an inescapable reality that the apostle Paul planted only multiethnic local churches. Paul was on mission to join the King of kings in fulfilling his covenant with Abraham. The apostle wrote: "The Scripture, foreseeing that God would justify the Gentiles by faith, preached the gospel beforehand to Abraham, saying, 'In you shall all the nations be blessed.' So then, those who are of faith are blessed along with Abraham, the man of faith" (Galatians 3:8–9). God promised Abraham a multiethnic family, and through faith in Jesus, this family would be realized on earth. Paul was turbocharged by God's grace and enabled by the Spirit to build churches like this throughout the first-century world. This was his passion. This was his mission. This is what landed him in prison.

Paul wrote, "For this reason I, Paul, a prisoner for Christ Jesus on behalf of you Gentiles—assuming that you have heard of the stewardship of God's grace that was given to me for you, how the mystery was made known to me by revelation, as I have written briefly" (Ephesians 3:1–3).

In essence, the apostle said, "I'm in prison because I'm reaching the Arabs, Greeks, Romans, barbarians, Asians, Africans, and other non-Jews to plant and build Jewish and Gentile local churches" (see Acts 21:17–36). If Paul were alive today in America, I believe he would say, "I'm on mission to reach Asian people, Latino people, Jewish people, White people, mixed-race people, and Black people! The gospel breaks down barriers and builds local churches in unity and reconciliation. I'm on a mission to fulfill God's covenant with Abraham."

Pastors and leaders, if the ministry environment you are in is ethnically diverse, are you developing Spirit-empowered ministry models to reach *all* the different people in your area as Paul did? I know we can't do this perfectly, but we can try.

Didn't Jesus die for all people equally? When we plant

homogeneous churches, it loudly proclaims that the ethnicities of people we target are more important than the other ethnicities in our ministry context. Just as Paul was a steward of God's grace, we, too, must steward God's grace and be on mission to reach all people in our communities.

WHAT IS THE MYSTERY OF CHRIST?

Paul then wrote: "When you read this, you can perceive my insight into the mystery of Christ, which was not made known to the sons of men in other generations as it has now been revealed to his holy apostles and prophets by the Spirit. This mystery is that the Gentiles are fellow heirs, members of the same body, and partakers of the promise in Christ Jesus through the gospel" (Ephesians 3:4–6).

The mystery is hinted at in the book of Isaiah:

> It shall come to pass in the latter days
> that the mountain of the house of the Lord
> shall be established as the highest of the mountains,
> and shall be lifted up above the hills;
> and all the nations shall flow to it,
> and many peoples shall come, and say:
> "Come, let us go up to the mountain of the Lord,
> to the house of the God of Jacob,
> that he may teach us his ways
> and that we may walk in his paths." (Isaiah 2:2–3)

Later the prophet said, "It is too light a thing that you should be my servant to raise up the tribes of Jacob and to bring back the preserved of Israel; I will make you as a light for the nations, that my salvation may reach to the end of the earth" (Isaiah 49:6).

It has always been in God's heart to create a reconciled, unified multiethnic family on earth, a creation only possible by Jesus the Messiah. The mystery of Christ is that, through the finished work of Jesus, a diverse family of God has been birthed into existence by the grace of God, a sign that God was faithful to keep his covenant with Abraham.

In Genesis 11, humanity was scattered and separated. In Genesis 12, God told Abraham that he would reconcile and unify humanity through him. This reconciliation and unification has been realized through Jesus the Messiah. In an act of amazing grace, the nations (Gentiles) became heirs along with Jews who trusted in Jesus. And not only that, they became members of the same body and partakers of the promise in Christ through the gospel. What is this promise? Paul wrote about that too:

> Remember that you [Gentiles] were at that time separated from Christ, alienated from the commonwealth of Israel and strangers to the *covenants of promise,* having no hope and without God in the world. But now in Christ Jesus you who once were far off have been brought near by the blood of Christ. (Ephesians 2:12–13, emphasis added)

The promise is that through the precious blood of Jesus, the Gentiles are now included in God's people, which are a new kind of people, a multiethnic people (see Ephesians 2:14–16).

I wonder if we, as pastors and leaders, really know this gospel reality. If we did, why would we continue to plant and maintain homogeneous churches? In my eighteen years as a Christ follower, I have never heard a sermon tie the gospel to God's keeping his covenant with Abraham, yet this biblical truth drives Paul in everything he did and said.

THE GOSPEL PAUL PREACHED

Under the Holy Spirit's inspiration, Paul wrote:

> Of this gospel I was made a minister according to the gift of God's grace, which was given me by the working of his power. To me, though I am the very least of all the saints, this grace was given, to preach to the Gentiles the unsearchable riches of Christ, and to bring to light for everyone what is the plan of the mystery hidden for ages in God who created all things. (Ephesians 3:7–9)

The apostle said, "Of this gospel I was made a minister according to the gift of God's grace." The gospel he preached did not permit him to plant and build homogeneous local churches. The gospel Paul preached was so powerful and beautiful that it fulfilled God's covenant promise to Abraham and produced multiethnic local churches. Paul preached that the Messiah's sinless life, substitutionary atoning death on the cross, glorious resurrection, and ascension created God's eternal purpose: multiethnic local churches.

Pastors and leaders, here's what's so beautiful: "the gift of God's grace" will work powerfully in us to become ambassadors of racial reconciliation and racial justice like the apostle Paul.

As you preach the "unsearchable riches of Christ," God himself will bring these to light for everyone to know the mystery: "Gentiles are fellow heirs, members of the same body, and partakers of the promise in Christ Jesus through the gospel" (Ephesians 3:6).

The "mystery of Christ," which Paul also calls the "mystery of faith," is so important Paul says church leaders and deacons (and elders) must hold firmly to the mystery of faith with a clear conscious (1 Timothy 3:8–9). This is a game changer.[1] Paul is saying you cannot be in church leadership unless you hold to building Jew/Gentile, multiethnic local churches with a clear conscience! Let's let God speak:

> Deacons likewise must be dignified, not double-tongued, not addicted to much wine, not greedy for dishonest gain. *They must hold the mystery of the faith with a clear conscience.* (1 Timothy 3:8–9 ESV, emphasis added)

The mystery of faith refers to Christ's work of bringing both Jews and Gentiles into one people of God (Ephesians 2:11–22; 3:6–9; Colossians 1:26; 3:11–16).[2] Jesus' epic salvific work creates a third ethnicity of people called the church. This new ethnicity is a multiethnic people who are one in Christ. This new ethnicity in Christ is a glimpse of eternity. The local churches in Ephesus were hope to the world that there is a better and more beautiful way to be human.

This interpretation makes perfect sense because Paul sent Timothy to oversee the churches in Ephesus:

> As I urged you when I was going to Macedonia, *remain at Ephesus so that you may charge certain persons not to teach any different*

doctrine, nor to devote themselves to myths and endless geneal-
ogies, which promote speculations rather than the stewardship
from God that is by faith. The aim of our charge is love that
issues from a pure heart and a good conscience and a sincere
faith. (1 Timothy 1:3–5 ESV, emphasis added)

Paul charged Timothy with protecting the doctrine of building Jew/Gentile churches or the "mystery of faith" in the churches
in Ephesus. And the aim of this community was love! What can
be more loving than Jews and Gentiles, former enemies, becoming
family in Christ and loving one another as an expression of God's
beautiful work of grace?

Paul dropped a thermal, global, nuclear, gospel bomb by saying
church leaders must hold to the mystery of faith or the mystery of
Christ, "which is that the Gentiles are fellow heirs, members of the
same body, and partakers of the promise in Christ Jesus through the
gospel. Of this gospel I was made a minister according to the gift
of God's grace, which was given me by the working of his power"
(Ephesians 3:6–8 ESV).

Paul just dropped the microphone. #Boom!

THE MANIFOLD WISDOM OF GOD AND WHY IT MATTERS

Paul said, "So that through the church the manifold wisdom
of God might now be made known to the rulers and authorities in
the heavenly places," and this was the "eternal purpose" realized in
Christ Jesus (Ephesians 3:10–11).

The apostle said that the Jew/Gentile multiethnic churches in

Ephesus declared the manifold wisdom of God to the rulers and authorities in heavenly places. The word *manifold* (Greek, *polupoikilos*) means many colored or rich variety.[3] Can you imagine the multicolored Jews, Africans, Greeks, barbarians, Asians, Spartans, Romans, and Arabs reading Paul's letter when it dawned on them that they are the multicolored wisdom of God to "rulers and authorities in the heavenly places," which includes angels and demons? This is practically the same picture Paul presented in Ephesians 2:21–22, when he said that Jews and Gentiles represented different-colored blocks in God's new temple, each color displaying God's glory. The multiethnic congregations in Ephesus proclaimed to the angels and demons that Jesus had won! God in Christ Jesus fulfilled his covenant with Abraham and gave Abraham his family. This gospel reality is still true today.

I want to warn you that building churches that reflect this diversity will bring suffering to your life. You will be ridiculed by other pastors and Christians. You will be discouraged and dismissed. There will be pastors and Christians who tell you, "Why don't you just preach the gospel?" You will experience significant spiritual warfare. I know because all of these have happened and are still happening to me. Why do you think Paul wrote about putting on the armor of God in the book of Ephesians? When you decide to commit to preaching the gospel that produces multiethnic local churches, spiritual warfare will heat up.

Spiritual Warfare and Suffering

The apostle wrote to the Ephesians from prison. Ultimately, planting these churches cost him his life. Planting multiethnic local churches is difficult, and you will suffer as well if you go down this path. Listen to Paul's words in Galatians 6:17: "I bear on my body the marks of Jesus."

Here's what Paul went through in order to build the church: he was imprisoned multiple times; he was beaten nearly to the point of death countless times; he was flogged, beaten with rods, stoned, shipwrecked, and spent a night adrift at sea; he faced dangers in rivers, dangers from robbers, danger from Jews and Gentiles, danger in the city and in the wilderness, and danger from false brothers; he spent multiple sleepless nights, was deprived of food and water, and nearly frozen to death. Paul was also burdened with the daily anxiety of caring for the multiethnic churches he planted. At one point he was even lowered through a window in a basket at night because the governor of Damascus wanted to arrest him (see 2 Corinthians 11:23–33). Paul suffered greatly planting ethnically diverse churches, just as the Lord Jesus said he would. After Paul's conversion, Jesus told his disciple Ananias: "He is a chosen instrument of mine to carry my name before the Gentiles and kings and the children of Israel. For I will show him how much he must suffer for the sake of my name" (Acts 9:15–16).

Maybe the reason the church in America is 86 percent homogeneous is because planting churches as the apostle Paul did is just too hard and great suffering is required.

God in Christ, through the Holy Spirit, is calling for the discipleship resurgence of ministry leaders like the apostle Paul to join Jesus in building his multiethnic church. Will you answer the call?

Jesus loves his church—the eternal purpose—and so should we.

THE CHURCH IS THE IDENTITY OF GOD'S PEOPLE

Jesus' church is not a weekend event; it's not a destination. The church is the identity of God's people. The Bible uses many metaphors to describe Jesus' church. I want to look at six. First, the church is called the bride of Christ (see Ephesians 5:32; 2 Corinthians 11:2); second, the church is the body of Christ (see 1 Corinthians 12:12–27); third, the church is God's royal priesthood (see 1 Peter 2:9–10); fourth, we are God's temple (see Ephesians 2:21–22); fifth, we are God's family (see 1 Timothy 5:1); and sixth, the church is a holy nation.

WE ARE THE BRIDE OF CHRIST

Isn't it beautiful that the Bible opens in Genesis with God creating Adam and his bride, Eve, and at the end, in Revelation, at the consummation of history, we find another husband named Jesus and his bride, the church: "'Let us rejoice and exult and give him the glory, for the marriage of the Lamb has come, and his Bride has made herself ready; it was granted her to clothe herself with fine linen, bright and pure'—for the fine linen is the righteous deeds of the saints" (Revelation 19:7–8).

Jesus is the last Adam and we, the church, are his bride, the new Eve (see 1 Corinthians 15:45; Romans 5:14). Just as a husband and wife are to be one, we, the bride of Christ, are united with our husband, Jesus. This gospel reality speaks of our union life in Christ. All that belongs to Jesus belongs to us by grace. We are the desire of his heart. His passion and affections have been lavished upon us.

To be one with Jesus means a life of intimacy. Jesus reveals himself to his bride. As we see him for who he is and all that he has done to win our hearts, we respond to him in love, loyalty, and obedience.

Picture this: Jesus was so lovesick, so passionate for us to behold his love, to behold his glory, to be his bride that he stepped out of eternity, stepped into time and space, and became a man. And he held nothing back from winning our hearts; he gave the ultimate price: his life. Jesus didn't approach us and say, "I have a diamond ring." He gave us the greatest treasure heaven could offer—himself.

Jesus makes his bride gloriously beautiful, holy, and without any blemishes (see Ephesians 5:25–27). Only Jesus' completed work can makes us beautiful. We are a perfect, multiethnic bride, despite our imperfect lives. Because Jesus is our great husband, his love covers the multitude of our sins.

Jesus' bride is globally multiethnic and should be present locally wherever possible.

WE ARE THE BODY OF CHRIST

Jesus is presently at the right hand of the Father, functioning as our great High Priest. This identity points to the gospel reality that Jesus' mission and ministry are continued on earth through his church. Every member of the body of Christ is needed and has a role to play. God values diversity, which is why he made such a variety of people.

Jesus' church is a collection of ethnically diverse people from all kinds of backgrounds with all kinds of gifts and abilities to bring glory to his name on earth. Multiethnic churches can become engines of innovation and creativity because of the diversity of the members of its congregations. Pastors and leaders, we have the sacred vocation of equipping God's people for the work of ministry. When this happens, each member grows and matures and Jesus' body is built up in love (see Ephesians 4:11–16).

WE ARE ROYAL PRIESTS

This gospel identity points to the reality that we, as God's people, collectively exist to worship Jesus in all of life (Romans 12:1–8). In Jewish theology, the temple is where heaven and earth met. The temple is where sins could be forgiven, in a room called the Holy of Holies, which contained the ark of the covenant. The temple would have been where the high priest, representing all of Israel, went behind a curtain into the Holy of Holies to make sacrifices on behalf of the people. The priest was the mediator between God and men. The priest, in essence, would hold the hand of the Jewish people and extend a hand to God the Father. This is a picture of Jesus, who is the great Mediator, our High Priest (see 1 Timothy 2:4–5). On the cross, Jesus grabbed the hand of humanity and the hand of God the Father, and on that cross he bridged the gap. In Latin, the word *priest* literally means "bridge builder." Jesus is the ultimate bridge builder, spanning the gap between people and God. Now, as God's royal priests, we continue his ministry today. The multiethnic church is about building bridges across ethnic and class boundaries to reach the lost, unredeemed people and to build up the believers.

WE ARE GOD'S TEMPLE

God has always longed to be with his people. In the cool mornings in the Garden of Eden, God walked with Adam. During the

Exodus, God's presence was signified by a pillar of cloud by day and a pillar of fire by night; God was with his people in a mobile tabernacle. Then God was with the people in the temple that Solomon built in Jerusalem. In the incarnation, God the Son was with us in flesh: "And the Word became flesh and dwelt among us, and we have seen his glory, glory as of the only Son from the Father, full of grace and truth" (John 1:14). And after Jesus' resurrection and ascension, Jews and Gentiles, the new people of God, became his new temple, the dwelling place of God. God is not only with us but in us. Each person represents a multicolored brick in this new temple that displays the glory of God:

> You are like a building that was built on the foundation of the apostles and prophets. Christ Jesus himself is the most important stone in that building, and that whole building is joined together in Christ. He makes it grow and become a holy temple in the Lord. And in Christ you, too, are being built together with the Jews into a place where God lives through the Spirit. (Ephesians 2:20–22 NCV)

What a stunningly beautiful picture. Imagine if we pastors, church planters, and denominational leaders allowed this gospel truth to shape how we lead our local churches.

WE ARE GOD'S FAMILY

God promised Abraham a multiethnic family, and through Jesus, God fulfilled his promise. When we choose to build and maintain homogeneous local churches in areas of ethnic diversity, we are basically saying to God, "I don't want to be with the rest of your children." But the gospel doesn't give us this option. If our churches are situated in communities of diversity, we are mandated by the gospel to be intentional about reaching everyone in all of the cultures around us. Let's reconsider the doctrine of justification and its implications.

Usually the doctrine of justification is taught to deal with an individual's personal sin. I am so grateful that the righteousness of Jesus is given to me as a gift. But my individual salvation and yours are so God's family can be formed. Individual salvation only exists so Jesus can have a bride called the church. Let's look at Galatians 3:24–29:

> So then, the law was our guardian until Christ came, in order that we might be justified by faith. But now that faith has come, we are no longer under a guardian, for in Christ Jesus you are all sons of God, through faith. For as many of you as were baptized into Christ have put on Christ. There is neither Jew nor Greek, there is neither slave nor free, there is no male and female, for you are all one in Christ Jesus. And if you are Christ's, then you are Abraham's offspring, heirs according to promise.

Paul was saying that Jews and Gentiles are declared righteous, not by works of the Law or by ethnicity (that is, being a Jew); they are declared righteousness because Jesus fulfilled the Law on their behalf. Jesus was faithful to the covenant. And now Jews and Gentiles are incorporated, baptized, and clothed in the Messiah himself. As a result, God has a multiethnic family of sons and daughters who treat each other equally, not based on ethnicity, social class, or gender, but on the basis of being clothed in Christ. The doctrine of justification confronts and condemns racism in the church, and if we truly grasp it, it will compel us to plant and build multiethnic local churches and transition homogeneous local churches into ethnically diverse churches.

WE ARE A HOLY NATION

The Greek word for "nation" is *ethnos,* meaning "ethnic groups." God told Abraham that he would make a great nation from him (see Genesis 12:1–3). This new multicolored nation was brought into being through the finished work of Jesus. And this nation was set apart, belonging to God and existing for God's purpose on the earth. This holy nation is a global family of diversity, and whenever possible, the gospel mandates that it is a local family of diversity. After Jesus' resurrection and ascension, a new group of humans populated the earth—a multiethnic, blood-bought, blood-covered people called the church, God's new, holy nation. God keeps his promises. He told Abraham he would do it, and he did. When we build ethnically diverse churches, we show that God keeps his word.

MULTIETHNIC CHURCHES ARE THE PRODUCT OF LOVE AND PRAYER

Planting, building, and maintaining multiethnic churches, as well as transitioning homogeneous churches into local multiethnic churches, was hard work in the first century, and it is hard work today. We need God's love to flood our hearts. His love is the superglue that brings different ethnicities together and creates churches from them. It's only his love that moves us beyond racism, prejudice, unforgiveness, and misunderstanding. And that's why Paul was inspired by the Holy Spirit to pen this prayer:

> For this reason I bow my knees before the Father, from whom every family in heaven and on earth is named, that according to the riches of his glory he may grant you to be strengthened with power through his Spirit in your inner being, so that Christ may dwell in your hearts through faith—that you, being rooted and grounded in love, may have strength to comprehend with all the saints what is the breadth and length and height and depth, and to know the love of Christ that surpasses knowledge, that you may be filled with all the fullness of God.
>
> Now to him who is able to do far more abundantly than all that we ask or think, according to the power at work within us, to him be glory in the church and in Christ Jesus throughout all generations, forever and ever. Amen. (Ephesians 3:14–21)

When you stay within the exegetical flow of what Paul wrote in this prayer, it is gorgeous and life giving. So often this prayer, especially verses 20–21, is used to raise money for capital campaigns or for some kind of "Jesus will make your dreams come true" sermon. This prayer for Paul was an encouragement to the churches of Ephesus that God's love would sustain and empower them to display God's manifold wisdom.

First, in reverence and worship, Paul said that God is the father of Jews and Gentiles in Christ. To be named by God means that he is your source of life and identity. God is not just the father of the Jews, he is father of the Gentiles also, and it is their togetherness that displays his faithfulness to fulfill his covenant (Ephesians 3:14–15).

Second, Paul prayed, according to the riches of God's glory, that Jews and Gentiles would be strengthened in their inner being by the Holy Spirit's power as the Messiah dwells in their hearts through faith and that they may be rooted and grounded in love (vv. 16–18). The apostle once again showed how their union life in the Messiah empowered them to love. It was God's love rooted and grounded in the Jews and Gentiles in Ephesus that sustained and grew the multiethnic local churches. This gospel reality is equally true today. It is our union life in the Messiah and faith in him that strengthens us to love each other. It's easy to love people who are just like us, but it takes faith and the strength of Jesus to love people who are different from us in a multiethnic local church environment.

Third, Paul prayed that these Jews and Gentiles in Ephesus would comprehend with all the saints the breadth and length and height and depth to know the love of the Messiah that surpasses all knowledge and to be filled with all the fullness of God (vv. 18–19). He essentially prayed, through the Spirit and their union life with Jesus, that God's love would fill them with all the fullness of God. This experience would transform them into the image of Jesus for the purpose of displaying God's manifold wisdom. Local multiethnic churches are for God's glory. And how do we know this to be true?

Fifth, Paul said to the Ephesian church and to us today that God is able to do more than we can think or even imagine, because he is working his mighty power within us (Ephesians 3:20–21)! And God wanted this to happen not just in the first century but today as well. Paul finished his prayer with a doxological flurry—"To him be glory in the church and in Christ Jesus throughout all generations, forever and ever. Amen" (v. 21).

It is only God's love and power that can build and sustain multi-ethnic local churches. They are God's design to end ethnic hatred and prejudice. The local church is God's school of love. Throughout the world, one of the great fears is ethnic hatred.[4] The answer to this fear is God's love and power in Christ through the Holy Spirit, which forms churches from various groups of people.

I believe the evil one is doing all he can to keep the church in America and the world divided along ethnic and class lines. He is waging war against God's manifold wisdom (see Ephesians 3:10). Paul knew and that's why he wrote to the churches at Ephesus about spiritual warfare in Ephesians 6:10–20.

IT'S WAR!

Like a wise father, Paul told the churches to be strong in the Lord (see Ephesians 6:10). Jesus himself is their strength. Jesus is the only one strong enough to defeat the evil one and his demonic forces. Then he told them to put on the whole armor of God so they could stand up to the schemes of the devil (see Ephesians 6:11–12). The devil doesn't want God to be faithful in fulfilling his covenant to Abraham. It was the devil who has always wanted to separate humanity from each other and from God. It is the devil who gave humans the idea to kill and enslave their fellow human beings.

The devil knows that homogeneous local churches *can* become hiding places for our prejudice, racism, and classism. But it is in doing life with others that these vile sins are revealed and healed. Paul used a Roman soldier as an illustration of God's armor: the belt of truth, the breastplate of righteousness, the shoes of the gospel, the shield of faith, the helmet of salvation, and the sword of the Spirit (the Word of God) (see Ephesians 6:14–18).

Paul clearly communicated why we need this armor when he wrote, "[Pray] also for me, that words may be given to me in opening my mouth boldly to proclaim the mystery of the gospel, for which I am an ambassador in chains, that I may declare it boldly, as I ought to speak" (Ephesians 6:19–20). The mystery of Christ "is that the Gentiles are fellow heirs, members of the same body, and partakers of the promise in Christ Jesus through the gospel. Of this gospel I was made a minister according to the gift of God's grace, which was given me by the working of his power" (Ephesians 3:6–7).

Paul fiercely and passionately built local multiethnic churches. Anything less would have been unimaginable. I think the apostle would look at the racially divided church in America and cry. He would say something like this: "The gospel I preached built communities of ethnic diversity that showcased the mystery of Christ and the manifold wisdom of God to the glory of God."

STUDY QUESTIONS, REFLECTIONS, AND PRAYER

1. Read Ephesians 3:6. What is the "mystery of Christ"? What are the implications of this for your local church?

2. Read Ephesians 3:8–10. What is God's "manifold wisdom"? What does he make this known through? What does this mean for your ministry?

3. Read Ephesians 3:10–12. What is God's "eternal purpose"? Who carried out this purpose?

4. In planting and building multiethnic churches, spiritual warfare and suffering will take a toll. Name the ways Paul suffered to plant multiethnic churches. Discuss the following statement as a team: *"Gospel-shaped leaders count the cost but move forward anyway, knowing that God's grace is sufficient to empower them to fulfill the task of planting multiethnic churches."*

5. Read Ephesians 3:14–21. How is this an example of how to pray for Jesus to plant and build his multiethnic church?

PRAYER

Father, you have an eternal purpose. May your purpose for local churches be our purpose too. Match our hearts with your heart. And give us your grace through the Spirit so we can partner in bringing you glory through your Son's bride, the church. In Jesus' name, amen.

EIGHT

SEEING DISCIPLESHIP AND LEADERSHIP THROUGH THE GOSPEL

Now these are the gifts Christ gave to the church: the apostles, the prophets, the evangelists, and the pastors and teachers. Their responsibility is to equip God's people to do his work and build up the church, the body of Christ. This will continue until we all come to such unity in our faith and knowledge of God's Son that we will be mature in the Lord, measuring up to the full and complete standard of Christ.

—EPHESIANS 4:11–13 NLT

DISCIPLESHIP AND CROSS-CULTURAL MINISTRY

Discipleship and cross-cultural ministry matter to Jesus. After Jesus defeated sin, death, and evil, he brought into being a new society, a new people of God made up of Jews and Gentiles. And as he was preparing to ascend to the right hand of the Father, he said to his disciples, "All authority in heaven and on earth has been given to me. Go therefore and make disciples of all nations, baptizing them in the name of the Father and of the Son and of the Holy Spirit, teaching them to observe all that I have commanded you. And behold, I am with you always, to the end of the age" (Matthew 28:18–20). Jesus restates the Great Commission a little differently in Acts 1:8: "But you will receive power when the Holy Spirit comes upon you, and you will be my witnesses in Jerusalem and in all Judea and Samaria, and to the ends of the earth" (NLT).

As first-century, second-temple Jews, those listening to his words "disciples of all nations" would have recalled the words of the prophets Isaiah and Zachariah and the psalmist concerning the salvation and inclusion of Gentiles into Israel.

Isaiah wrote, "It is too light a thing that you should be my servant to raise up the tribes of Jacob and to bring back the preserved of Israel; I will make you as a light for the nations, that my salvation may reach to the end of the earth" (Isaiah 49:6).

Zechariah wrote, "And many nations shall join themselves to the LORD in that day, and shall be my people. And I will dwell in your midst, and you shall know that the LORD of hosts has sent me to you" (Zechariah 2:11).

And the psalmist wrote: "For this I will praise you, O LORD, among the nations, and sing to your name. Great salvation he brings to his king, and shows steadfast love to his anointed, to David and his offspring forever," and "Praise the LORD, all nations! Extol him, all peoples! For great is his steadfast love toward us, and the faithfulness of the LORD endures forever. Praise the LORD!" (Psalms 18:49–50; 117:1–2).

Deeply rooted within the story of Israel has always been a passion to reach the nations (the Gentiles) so they could receive salvation and be included in God's people.

God made a covenant with Abraham, and his steadfast love revealed in the person of Jesus has fulfilled the covenant through the mystery of Christ: "Both Gentiles and Jews who believe the Good News share equally in the riches inherited by God's children. Both are part of the same body, and both enjoy the promise of blessings because they belong to Christ Jesus" (Ephesians 3:6 NLT). This is God's eternal purpose, his manifold wisdom that proclaims his victory to the angelic and demonic realms (see Ephesians 3:9–12; Revelation 5:9–12).

NOT A COINCIDENCE

It's a not a coincidence that after Christ's birth his parents fled to Egypt and later returned to the Promised Land from Egypt, just like the nation of Israel (see Matthew 2:13–14). It's not a coincidence that Israel was called God's son ("Out of Egypt I called my son") and Jesus is the Son of God (see Hosea 11:1; Matthew 16:16). It's not a coincidence that Jesus went through the waters of baptism in the Jordan, reflecting the nation of Israel crossing the Red Sea (see Matthew 3:17; 4:1–11).

It's not a coincidence that Jesus spent forty days in the wilderness being tempted by the devil and all three temptations reflected Israel's experience in the wilderness. (See Deuteronomy 6:13, 16;

8:3.) These temptations also correspond to how the evil one tempted Adam and Eve in the garden (Genesis 3:1, 4–5).

It's not a coincidence that at Jesus' birth, Zechariah said, "Lord, now you are letting your servant depart in peace, according to your word; for my eyes have seen your salvation that you have prepared in the presence of all peoples, a light for revelation to the Gentiles, and for glory to your people Israel" (Luke 2:29–32).

Jesus is the New Israel, the New Jacob, and the twelve disciples correspond to the twelve tribes of Israel (see Matthew 10:1–4). Through the disciples, Jesus resurrected Israel's sacred vocation of being the light to the nations. He was establishing the New Israel that would include Gentiles. The apostle Paul also communicated this gospel reality: "For neither circumcision counts for anything, nor uncircumcision, but a new creation. And as for all who walk by this rule, peace and mercy be upon them, and upon the Israel of God" (Galatians 6:15–16). And he added that Jesus "made peace between Jews and Gentiles by creating in himself one new people from the two groups. Together as one body, Christ reconciled both groups to God by means of his death on the cross, and our hostility toward each other was put to death" (Ephesians 2:15–16 NLT). And this new multiethnic Israel is now God's dwelling place, God's new temple imaging forth his glory (see Ephesians 2:21–22).

Israel was set free from slavery in Egypt to be the corporate Adam, thus fulfilling the mission God gave to Adam. After the Exodus, God said to the people:

> You yourselves have seen what I did to the Egyptians, and how
> I bore you on eagles' wings and brought you to myself. Now

therefore, if you will indeed obey my voice and keep my covenant, you shall be my treasured possession among all peoples, for all the earth is mine; and you shall be to me a kingdom of priests and a holy nation. (Exodus 19:4–6)

The apostle Peter uses the same language to describe the church:

But you are a chosen race, a royal priesthood, a holy nation, a people for his own possession, that you may proclaim the excellencies of him who called you out of darkness into his marvelous light. Once you were not a people, but now you are God's people; once you had not received mercy, but now you have received mercy. (1 Peter 2:9–10)

So now the church exists to join Jesus in creating local congregations throughout the world that reveal the mystery of Christ as a proclamation of God's faithfulness to Abraham.

WHAT'S THE POINT?

Jesus' early disciples would have viewed an essential aspect of discipleship as cross-cultural engagement with Gentiles so God's multiethnic church could fill the earth. God was so serious about the mystery of Christ being displayed on earth that when the early disciples stayed in Jerusalem and Judea, proclaiming the gospel only to Jews instead of going on mission to Samaria and to the ends of the earth, the Lord allowed persecution to force them beyond their homeland so the Gentiles could experience the salvation of the Lord and inclusion into God's new Israel (see Acts 8:1)!

DISCIPLESHIP AND THE MYSTERY OF CHRIST

Often our models of discipleship in America have absolutely nothing to do with the mystery of Christ and partnering with God in establishing his eternal purpose on earth. Our discipleship tends to be primarily about personal holiness through spiritual disciplines. Spiritual disciplines and personal holiness are wonderful things; however, God the Holy Spirit longs to conform us to the image of Jesus so we can reveal the mystery of Christ as a sign of God's faithfulness. The apostle Paul asserted:

> To them God chose to make known how great among the Gentiles are the riches of the glory of this mystery, which is Christ in you, the hope of glory. Him we proclaim, warning everyone and teaching everyone with all wisdom, that we may present everyone mature in Christ. For this I toil, struggling with all his energy that he powerfully works within me. (Colossians 1:27–29)

According to Paul, he toiled and struggled to teach everyone (Jew and Gentile) in Colossi with wisdom so all could be mature in Christ. In this context, Paul defined maturity as "to make known how great among the Gentiles are the riches of the glory of this mystery, which is Christ in you, the hope of glory" (v. 27). For the apostle, maturity in Christ was associated with joining God in filling the earth with the mystery of Christ. The mystery of Christ was God's answer to humanity's ethnic hostility and division. The mystery of Christ is about unifying and reconciling humanity, bringing God's justice and peace to earth.

I received a letter recently that serves as a good example of why God desires to fill the earth with multiethnic local churches of unity and reconciliation:

> I am the youth pastor. Our church struggles with racism. I have been at the church for ten years, and I have wanted to leave, but God is telling me to stay. I have been attacked numerous times for black kids coming to church with me. I also teach and coach at the local public high school. I just left a board meeting at my church where members of my church came in and attacked me again for trying to divide the church. They were saying black people worship different than whites and we don't want them to come take over the church. The majority of the board members agree with me, and the preacher believes all are welcome to worship with us. When I was getting attacked by Satan tonight, you came to mind. Will you please pray for me and our church? Right now we have two African Americans that attend our church regularly, and I don't want them to be attacked or get discouraged.

If our philosophy of discipleship is dislodged from God's people partnering with him in fulfilling his covenant to Abraham, then we have a *truncated* philosophy of discipleship. I'm not saying it's wrong. I am saying that based on God's eternal purpose, which is the mystery of Christ, then, yes, it is an underdeveloped philosophy of discipleship, which leads to homogeneous local churches and an individualized faith that is more about a person rather than God's glory.

Now, if you are in an area where your demographics do not support your goal of diversity, then another means of seeing this gospel reality must be pursued. So what does that look like for you and the local church you serve?

DISCIPLESHIP: LOVE GOD AND LOVE ALL PEOPLE THE WAY YOU LOVE YOURSELF

Jesus cast the greatest discipleship vision for humanity ever when he communicated the Great Commandment and the Great Commission (see Luke 10:25–29; Matthew 28:18–20). As I shared earlier, the vision of Transformation Church is rooted in these two great commandments. Our vision is that "we are a multiethnic, multigenerational, mission-shaped community that loves God completely (Upward), ourselves correctly (Inward), and our neighbors compassionately (Outward)." The first part of the vision is rooted in the Great Commission, and the latter part of the vision is rooted in the Great Commandment. In response to God's unsearchable riches in Christ, by the Spirit's enablement, we are to grow in loving God completely, in loving ourselves correctly, and in loving our neighbors compassionately. Our neighbors here are multiethnic and multigenerational.

Jesus not only cast the vision for discipleship, but God himself is the *provision* to embody the vision: "Now to him who is able to do far more abundantly than all that we ask or think, according to the power at work within us, to him be glory in the church and in Christ Jesus throughout all generations, forever and ever. Amen"

(Ephesians 3:20–21). God's vision, if received by faith, restores humanity to its original purpose while at the same time building God's eternal purpose, which is the mystery of Christ—namely, local multiethnic churches. These churches can become communities of love, reconciliation, and unity. These communities are a model for the world to see humanity at its best. They are agents of transformation.

DEVELOP A DISCIPLESHIP STRATEGY

I strongly encourage pastors, especially young pastors, to spend time thinking through a biblical philosophy and a strategy of discipleship. As I engage pastors on this topic, I find many younger pastors are concerned with creating weekend worship experiences. Jesus' bride is more than a well-produced weekend service with laser light shows, smoke machines, and viral videos. I'm not against creativity; Transformation Church has a creative weekend service. What I am against is not having a well-developed philosophy and strategy of biblical discipleship. Why are you doing what you do? How is it moving the local church forward toward God's eternal purpose? Having a large crowd on the weekend is not a church, but the crowd has the potential to become one. A biblical discipleship strategy can move the crowd into becoming a local church.

Now, on the flip side, we live in a modern age, and our weekend services should reflect the times in which we live. We need thoroughly biblical, Christ-centered, doxological weekend services that connect with people who live in the modern era, not 1976 or 1876. Our God is the creator of three hundred billion galaxies and displays limitless creativity; therefore, as his image bearers, we long for creativity as well. We should seek to proclaim the timeless truth of the gospel in a timely way.

THE NAME "TRANSFORMATION CHURCH"

In a New Testament class in 2004, I was studying Romans 12:1–2:

> I appeal to you therefore, brothers, by the mercies of God, to present your bodies as a living sacrifice, holy and acceptable to God, which is your spiritual worship. Do not be conformed to this world, but be transformed by the renewal of your mind, that by testing you may discern what is the will of God, what is good and acceptable and perfect.

I thought, *That's it! God wants to transform us!* As God's people look back at his mercy in Christ, we become living sacrifices and all of life becomes worship. We are transformed from the inside out. Transformation can only take place when, by the Holy Spirit's power, Christ in us lives through us and we become living sacrifices for the glory of God.

THE FIVE CHARACTERISTICS OF A DISCIPLE

As my wife, Vicki, our friends Angela and Paul, and I turned our dining room into the Transformation Church offices in the summer of 2009, we prayed and fasted about a biblical approach to discipleship. What would disciples look like? What characteristics would mark their life? After months of prayer and fasting, in addition to all my years of study and theological reflection since 1997, we concluded that New Testament disciples demonstrated five characteristics: worship, connection, servanthood, giving, and living missionally.

At our church, we call ourselves transformers because, in Christ, we are empowered by the Spirit to be agents of transformation and ambassadors of reconciliation. We teach that the five characteristics of a disciple, or a transformer, are

1. Seeing all of life as worship.
2. Connecting in small groups.
3. Serving in the local church and in the world through our vocations.
4. Giving generously to the local church.
5. Living as missionaries in the everydayness of life as we invite lost people into our spheres of influence to know Jesus.

Let's look at each characteristic closely.

Worship

As a man, Jesus lived in constant communion and union with his Father (see John 5:17–24; 10:30). Jesus is God's prototype for humanity; Jesus lived as humanity was created and designed to live—in complete dependence on the Holy Spirit (see Luke 4:16–19). And now that we, by faith, have received Jesus, we live in union life with him. We are in communion and union with Jesus. Therefore, all of life is worship as we abide in Christ, participate in Christ, and live as God's temple. Jesus said, "I am the vine; you are the branches. If you remain in me and I in you, you will bear much fruit; apart from me you can do nothing" (John 15:5 NIV), and the apostle Peter said, "So that through them you may become partakers of the divine nature" (2 Peter 1:4). Finally, the apostle Paul said, "Do you not know that you are God's temple and that God's Spirit dwells in you?" (1 Corinthians 3:16).

At Transformation Church, we are attempting to equip people to worship our tri-person God in all of life by abiding in Christ, by participating in Christ, walking in the Spirit, and by understanding that they are God's temple. We are living, breathing, individual houses of worship that collectively build God's temple.

We are strategically equipping transformers through our incorporation process, preaching, and small groups, and through the sacred vocations of school, work, and play. When we are abiding in Christ, participating in Jesus' life, and seeing ourselves as God's temple, all of life becomes God's sacred playground of worship.

Along with pulpit preaching, our incorporation process begins with several events that invite people to learn more about what discipleship looks like in action. We begin with a newcomer meeting, where we introduce our mission, our vision, and our staff. This is followed by an invitation to learn more at three pathway classes, which are "Who We Are," "How We Live," and "Who You Are." Finally, those who wish to make Transformation their church home will attend a covenant class, which leads to membership.

CONNECT

Because our triune God is a community of love, God's people are created for connection. One of the ways we attempt to equip and disciple the transformer community is through our small-group ministry called Transformation Groups (TC Groups). First, our TC Groups are multiethnic and multigenerational. It is common to have TC Groups with babies, teenagers, young adults, all the way up through people in their eighties! Cultural and age diversity generate great conversation, organic mentoring, and discipleship.

We don't have women-only or men-only TC Groups. We believe that husbands and wives need to be in community to discuss the Scriptures together. I've heard men say, "I need a men's group because there are certain things I can't say around my wife." And I respond, "Well, that's why your marriage will never have deep intimacy. You are one flesh with your wife, not Steve and Bart in your men's group." Our life is so fast-paced, with so little time for connection, so it's important for husbands and wives to be together, not separated.

We believe it's important for those who are single and those who are married to be in the same TC Groups also. Singles are not incomplete if they don't have a spouse. Single people can actually accomplish more for God's kingdom than married people because they don't have a spouse to look after. We need to give our singles in the church the dignity of being treated as equal to married people. Singles are married to Jesus; they, too, are the bride of Christ.

We believe that God's people mature in the faith in the context of multiethnic, multigenerational relationships. Learning from the diversity of various cultures and stages of life is essential to developing a community that can help God display the mystery of Christ. For example, what is a group of twenty-one-year-old guys going to teach each other? Whereas, when you are with men and women of different ages and stages of life, diversity creates natural mentoring relationships. We all learn from each other.

Our groups' study questions are based on the previous weekend's sermon. We want our people thoroughly soaked in God's Word. There are several advantages to having people study questions derived from the sermon.

1. Creating those questions makes me a better preacher and our congregation better implementers of the sermon. What sense does it make to spend twenty-plus hours a week preparing a sermon that people will listen to for forty-five minutes and then forget? In study questions derived from the sermon, our people interact, discuss, and look for ways to apply what's been preached.
2. It keeps everyone moving in the same direction of embodying the vision.
3. Everyone teaches others in the group because the facilitator encourages conversations. This empowers everyone to have gospel conversations, which helps them grow in articulating their faith.
4. As a unified church, we are learning biblical and systematic theology together.

In our groups, we are able to pray for one another, keep one another accountable, serve our city and world together, and do life with each other. My wife and I do not lead the TC Group we are in; we are pastored by the group and others. And we love it.

SERVE

In many churches, one of the biggest missing elements of discipleship or maturity in Christ is serving in local church ministry. When we serve in local church ministry, we are not only following the example of Jesus, but we are growing in other-centeredness instead of self-centeredness. On the night Jesus was betrayed, his disciples argued about who was the greatest, and Jesus washed their feet to show them what true greatness looked like (see Luke 22:24–27). In the midst of their sin, Jesus, the eternal Son of God, did what the lowest slave of a household would have done by washing the feet of disciples. And then he said,

> You call me Teacher and Lord, and you are right, for so I am.
> If I then, your Lord and Teacher, have washed your feet, you
> also ought to wash one another's feet. For I have given you an
> example, that you also should do just as I have done to you. Truly,
> truly, I say to you, a servant is not greater than his master, nor is a
> messenger greater than the one who sent him. If you know these
> things, blessed are you if you do them. (John 13:13–17)

We are blessed when we serve others, and local church ministry is a discipleship instrument that blesses the child of God and builds up the local church in love. I often say at the weekend service, "If your idea of belonging to a local church is sitting in a seat week after week while others serve you, you're not going to like our community. We are a community of servants, and everyone is needed to help us fulfill our calling as a local church. One of the core values of Transformation Church is that 'we are committed, by the Spirit's enabling power, to develop a biblical, servant-hearted community in which we serve each other through our grace gifts as we serve in our spheres of influence by being the heart, hands, and feet of Jesus.'"[1]

The apostle Paul wrote:

> Now these are the gifts Christ gave to the church: the apostles, the prophets, the evangelists, and the pastors and teachers. Their responsibility is to equip God's people to do his work and build up the church, the body of Christ. . . .
>
> He makes the whole body fit together perfectly. As each part does its own special work, it helps the other parts grow, so that the whole body is healthy and growing and full of love. (Ephesians 4:11–12, 16 NLT)

It is the responsibility of the elder pastors to equip God's people for the work of ministry, and their collective work together builds up the church in love. We would be hurting God's people and diminishing the glory of the mystery of Christ if we did not move transformers toward service in the local church within our ministry matrix.

We also have an amazing care team led by Pastor Paul Allen and Denise Covert, our TC care director. Denise came to Transformation Church hurt and wounded, but she now leads an army of lay ministers who walk alongside church members who have marriage issues, financial issues, are in substance abuse recovery, or struggling with other concerns. Our care team, along with the other elders, pastors, and me, carry the load of shepherding God's people at Transformation Church. This is another example of discipleship and service going hand in hand.

We also believe that if our equipping and training of transformers in local church ministry does not empower them to do their jobs more effectively, then we've failed. We believe that vocations—from jobs to school—are a means to serve our world.

GIVE

Another aspect of discipleship that is often neglected is financial generosity. The deeper we've experienced the grace of God, the deeper we dig into our wallets in sacrificial generosity toward the local church so others can experience the grace of God. The deeper we have experienced the grace of God, the deeper we shift our lives to free up financial resources to give to the local church and other Christ-centered ministries to introduce people to the unsearchable riches of Christ.

At Transformation Church, we teach a theology of generosity, not tithing. We believe that 10 percent giving is the elementary school of generosity. Grace should move us well beyond the tithe. When the apostle Paul was taking up an offering for the church in Jerusalem, he motivated Macedonian believers with these words, "For you know the grace of our Lord Jesus Christ, that though he was rich, yet for your sake he became poor, so that you by his poverty might become rich" (2 Corinthians 8:9).

I'll never forget the day my wife and I called our then-teenage daughter and preteen son into the kitchen. We shared with them that in order to plant Transformation Church we would have to give away a lot of money and that it would change the way we lived. My daughter asked, "Dad, if we do this, how will I get a car?" I said, "Baby, I'm not sure, but we are going to trust God to provide."

I knew that if I wanted Transformation Church to bleed financial generosity toward God's kingdom, Vicki and I needed to hemorrhage it. Over the last five years, the people of Transformation Church are growing in financial generosity toward God's kingdom because they are growing in grace. Oh, and my daughter was able to get a car on her seventeenth birthday. God provides.

Jesus said, "Wherever your treasure is, there the desires of your heart will also be" (Matthew 6:21 NLT). If you want to know if someone is growing in grace and growing in discipleship, look at how they spend their money and their habits of giving to the local church and other Christ-centered ministry.

This aspect of discipleship is so important that we designed a class taught by financial advisors who are church members to help our people learn biblical stewardship. The reality is that God doesn't need our money. Giving isn't for God; giving is for us. As we learn to give sacrificially and generously to God's kingdom, we loosen the idolatrous grip of greed and tighten our grip of faith on Jesus.

INVITE

Finally, we equip our people to be missionaries. We believe every Christ follower is a missionary and shaped by the mission of Jesus. This means we are equipping the church to see that God's mission is the driving force behind our actions, individually and corporately. Our vocations, meaning our jobs or schools, become our mission fields. We teach people to pray for, care for, and share their grace stories (testimonies) with the lost people in their lives. As relationships of love and trust are built, transformers invite their lost friends to weekend services and TC groups.

Being a missionary is simply the outflow of loving our neighbors compassionately because God first loved us. The greatest thing we can ever do for other human beings is to introduce them to Jesus Christ. At Transformation Church, I say, "I've never led anyone to Christ. But God the Holy Spirit has used me in conjunction with all of you to lead people to Jesus." As we build relationships with lost people, we are tilling the soil of their hearts, we are planting seeds of grace, we are watering the seeds, and then God brings about a harvest.

Because we are mission-shaped, our services are both attractional and missional. Throughout the week, transformers are on mission, and on the weekend, whoever is preaching will preach in a way that nonbelievers will understand without dumbing down the gospel. We believe that lost people need Jesus, and we believe that found people need Jesus. We believe that the same gospel that justifies the sinners will sanctify and glorify the saints.

We are a young church, so we are continually learning. But we do know that a discipleship philosophy and strategy rooted in the Great Commandment and the Great Commission and reliance on the power of God's great grace will create local multiethnic churches that become agents of transformation.

LEADERSHIP DEVELOPMENT

On every football team I played for from middle school to the NFL, I've been nominated as a team captain. And every successful football team I played on had effective leadership. As the leaders of the team went, so went the team. When God rescued me and birthed me into his family, I learned that the church stands or falls on the shoulders of *her* leaders as well.

I believe the best leaders in the world should be in pastoral ministry. I believe this because it is the pastoral leadership team's responsibility to equip God's people for the work of ministry through their sacred vocations. I knew that in order for Transformation Church to fulfill her calling, I needed humble, gifted, smart people who love Jesus and his church to serve alongside me.

If I am the smartest and most gifted person in the leadership room, my rooms are too small or I'm too insecure to serve with people who are more gifted and smarter than I am. As I asked God to bring me a great leadership team in the summer of 2009, I wanted people who were more gifted, smarter, and who had more ministry experience than I did. God answered my prayers, bringing me Tim Jordan and Paul Allen.

In the fall of 2009, I was driving Vicki and Angela crazy. I knew what God wanted to do through Transformation Church, and I also knew my leadership inadequacies, and it produced fear. But in his grace, God had me attend a church planters' retreat where two Christian psychologists flayed my heart wide open and exposed all my fears, doubts, and insecurities. For two days, I called my wife weeping, confessing, and repenting of trying to build Jesus' church. It was as if the Holy Spirit gave me the okay not to be able to do everything. As I released my fears, God brought Tim Jordan to our team. Tim is the salt of the earth. At the time, he was in his late fifties. He had experience running the operations of a four-thousand-member church. Then God brought Paul, who also was in his late fifties, and he had experience as an executive pastor of a ten-thousand-member church. Paul is an experienced, witty, and loyal man. With Tim and Paul on board, I was freed up to do what I do best: pray, cast vision, study God's Word, preach, and build teams. Tim, Paul, Angela, and Vicki built the infrastructure of Transformation Church.

While on the retreat, I drew this picture of how I wanted our leadership team to live and function and how I wanted it to give life and leadership development to Transformation Church and beyond. We would create tight-knit circles of Upward, Inward, Outward people, and out of these circles of love, thousands upon thousands, dare I say millions, will be transformed by God's vision for Transformation Church.

Next, I knew that Transformation Church needed to have a pipeline of leadership development; therefore, we needed to create a leadership development strategy. We needed to define the characteristics of leaders as well. We view Transformation Church in four circles: the community, the congregation, the committed, and the core.[2] The community is anyone who has attended a worship service on the weekend; the congregation is anyone who has attended services for a couple of months; the committed are those who embody the five characteristics of a disciple; and the core are people who not only embody the five characteristics but have also gone through our covenant class and have agreed to be covenant partners with Transformation Church.

Our goal is to progressively move people from community to congregation to committed to core. For the committed and core, we have leadership development gatherings led by our ministry directors. These gatherings are focused on our vision, values, emotionally healthy spirituality, and a competency skill that will equip them to function in their ministry roles in Transformation Church and in their sacred vocations in the marketplace. The staff of Transformation Church has grown from three to more than thirty in five years, and the great majority of our staff has come out of the leadership development gatherings.

THE FIVE CHARACTERISTICS OF A LEADER

As we are developing leaders for staff and other ministry areas at Transformation Church, we want to build the five C's into our perspective leaders. The five C's are character, competency, catalytic, collaboration, and chemistry.[3]

CHARACTER

We are partnering with the Holy Spirit to identify and cultivate people of character. God's church must be served and shepherded by people of deep godly character. At Transformation Church, when we say character, we mean the fruit of the Spirit: "The fruit of the Spirit is love, joy, peace, patience, kindness, goodness, faithfulness, gentleness, self-control; against such things there is no law. And those who belong to Christ Jesus have crucified the flesh with its passions and desires" (Galatians 5:22–24). Only a person who is walking in the Spirit and who belongs to Jesus can display this type of character.

COMPETENCY

If a person is called to leadership at Transformation Church at any level, we give them a clear ministry role description and equip them to fulfill that role. Any ambiguity and lack of equipping sets people up to fail. Sadly, we've done this and we've had to repent. People get hurt when they are confused about a ministry role and are not equipped to fulfill their task. We want people to flourish for the glory of God in their ministry roles. And being equipped is vital for flourishing.

CATALYTIC

We are looking for and developing people who are catalytic. For us, this means people who take the initiative on projects. You have to tell them to slow down, because they are trying to make something happen. They are movers of men and women toward the vision. They have a humble confidence about them. A catalytic person generates ideas, innovation, and comes up with solutions to problems. A catalytic person has potential for growth. Catalytic people also reproduce themselves.

COLLABORATION

Collaboration is essential to any healthy, effective organization. Two Derwinisms of Transformation Church are "Teamwork makes

the dream work" and "TEAM: Together Everyone Achieves More."
When people on a team are not willing to collaborate, it usually
means that underneath this lack of sharing lies insecurity. Some
people have used information as a weapon to control others or as
an insurance policy so they will always have their ministry role. I
say that one of the ways to guarantee your ministry is to reproduce
other leaders, increase organizational health through collaboration,
and never forget: do not attach your identity to a ministry role;
attach it to Jesus. Your ministry role may change, but your identity
in Christ is unchanging, and this gospel reality gives us the power
to collaborate because we are secure in Christ.

CHEMISTRY

Finally, the local church is a family, not a business. We desire
that our staff and other ministry leaders like and love each other, not
just function as colleagues. God's church is a family; this speaks of
relationship and intimacy. I want to serve Transformation Church
with friends—brothers and sisters who love and respect each other.
Therefore, conflict resolution and emotionally healthy leadership
are very important to me and the other elder pastors. We want the
healthiest members of Transformation Church to be our leaders
because healthy leaders reproduce healthy leaders who produce a
healthy congregation through the Holy Spirit's power.

Every Tuesday morning we have Transformation Time, where I
or one of the other elder pastors shepherd the staff through how to
live and lead out of the gospel of grace. I desire that we are a beautiful, healthy, spiritually mature leadership team. For as we go, so
goes Transformation Church.

DISCIPLESHIP AND LEADERSHIP DEVELOPMENT

Discipleship and leadership development are critical to local churches fulfilling their calling as agents of transformation. Therefore, gospel-formed leaders are committed to a discipleship philosophy that is rooted in creating local congregations throughout America and the world that reveal the mystery of Christ as a sign and foretaste of God's faithfulness to Abraham and of Jesus' victory.

God's eternal purpose—the mystery of Christ, which is multiethnic local congregations that are learning to love and embody reconciliation and unity—is literally the hope of the world. The mystery of Christ is a witness to the world of what life with God looks like.

STUDY QUESTIONS, REFLECTIONS, AND PRAYER

1. *"Discipleship and cross-cultural ministry matter to Jesus."* What does this statement mean to you and your ministry?
2. How do you define discipleship? Read Colossians 1:27–29. What is the role in discipleship of spiritual disciplines? of personal holiness? of the mystery of Christ? of God's eternal purpose?
3. Do you or your church have a discipleship strategy? Can you articulate it? What steps can you take to make it more clear and applicable?

4. Does your church have a strategy for leadership development? Describe it. If you don't, what are some steps you can take this week to begin to develop one or have conversations with your pastor about the need for it at your church?

5. Discuss the following statement as a team: *"Gospel-shaped leaders are committed to developing and implementing a strategy of leadership development."* Why would this be important to your church?

PRAYER

Father, in the finished work of Jesus, by and through the gracious work of the Spirit, give us knowledge of how to develop disciples and leaders. Do this for your glory, Lord, the joy of our staff and congregation, and for the sake of the lost. In Jesus' name, amen.

NINE

SEEING THE WORLD
TO COME

And I saw the holy city, the new Jerusalem,
coming down from God out of heaven like a
bride beautifully dressed for her husband.
—REVELATION 21:2 NLT

BEGIN WITH THE END IN MIND

Effective leaders know you can't lead a people if you don't know where you are going. And you can't lead anyone where you haven't been yourself. The God of Abraham, Isaac, and Jacob had the end in mind when he created image bearers to show his glory and love on planet earth.

The apostle John wrote about God's eternal purpose for humanity:

And they sang a new song, saying,

> "Worthy are you to take the scroll
> and to open its seals,
> for you were slain, and by your blood you ransomed
>> people for God
> from every tribe and language and people and nation,
> and you have made them a kingdom and priests to
>> our God,
> and they shall reign on the earth."

Then I looked, and I heard around the throne and the living creatures and the elders the voice of many angels, numbering myriads of myriads and thousands of thousands, saying with a loud voice,

> "Worthy is the Lamb who was slain
> to receive power and wealth and wisdom and might
> and honor and glory and blessing!" (Revelation 5:9–12)

God, who lives in the eternal now and who knows the end from the beginning, has envisioned a regenerated, justified, reconciled, unified, multiethnic family in the Messiah. For all time, the Father, the Son, and the Holy Spirit have seen this family to be a kingdom of priests who sing a new song to Jesus. Think about what this new song will sound like and how our hearts will burst with infinite, *eptastic* joy? If we, as the not-yet-glorified people of God, can make beautiful music now, imagine the coming eternal day when we sing to the Lamb who is worthy of our new song! Can you hear the melody? Can you hear how our diverse cultural musical expressions through our voices and the playing of instruments will make a sound like we've never heard before? This new song will display our love, adoration, joy, and unity in Jesus.

I long for that hopeful day. And so do the Father, the Son, and the Holy Spirit.

God longs for this day so much that Jesus substituted himself on the cross in humanity's place and became sin so we could experience God's love. He did this so we can be forgiven, be redeemed, be declared the very righteous of God, and be reconciled to God and each other.

God longs for this day with such an ache in his heart that he raised Jesus from the dead so we, his multiethnic people, could share and participate in Jesus' life. God longs for this day with a hunger so unstoppable that Jesus ascended to his Father's right hand and now intercedes on behalf of his people as the great High Priest.

God longs for this day so much that he sent the Holy Spirit to regenerate, sanctify, gift, and bear fruit in his people, to send them on mission to build local multiethnic churches wherever possible to the glory of God.

God is so passionate about the church because it is his covenant people, the body of Christ, who carry on Jesus' ministry and mission. If the world wants to know what Jesus is like, the church is called and empowered to be a mosaic of Jesus' beautiful face. Just like the multiethnic church in Corinth, we are called and empowered to love each other (see 1 Corinthians 13:4–8).

TODAY CAN BE A FORETASTE OF THAT GREAT ETERNAL DAY

I love Pappadeaux Seafood Kitchen, which specializes in Cajun seafood. When you walk into a Pappadeaux, the spicy scent makes your mouth water. My favorite appetizer is oysters Pappadeaux—baked oysters on the half shell with crabmeat, spinach, and hollandaise. After I eat this culinary masterpiece, I long for the full-course meal!

Pastors and leaders, the local church is to be a mouth-watering foretaste of the full-course meal to come (see Revelation 5:9–12; 21:1–4). According to God, the eternal church will be a multiethnic church of love, reconciliation, unity, and celebration of Jesus, so we are called to join Jesus to make that a reality today. Our individual salvation is to point to a greater, more beautiful story. It's the story of God's glory revealed in his multiethnic church and unified in his eternal Son, the Lord Jesus.

GOD'S ETERNAL PURPOSE: THE MYSTERY OF CHRIST

God, the eternal One, has always had an end goal in mind for his creation. The apostle Paul called God's end goal the "eternal purpose":

> To me, though I am the very least of all the saints, this grace was given, to preach to the Gentiles the unsearchable riches of Christ, and to bring to light for everyone what is the plan of the mystery hidden for ages in God who created all things, so that through the church the manifold wisdom of God might now be

made known to the rulers and authorities in the heavenly places.
This was according to the eternal purpose that he has realized in
Christ Jesus our Lord. (Ephesians 3:8–11)

What is God's eternal purpose? According to Paul, it is the "manifold wisdom of God" (see Ephesians 3:10). As we learned earlier,
manifold means "rich variety" or "multicolored." So when the Jews
and ethnically diverse Gentiles from the known world—as far west
as Spain, as far north as Northern Europe, as far east as the Middle
East, and as far south as North Africa—read Paul's letters, they could
physically see their rich variety or multicoloredness and unity displayed to the angelic and demonic realm that Jesus had won![1]

In an ethnically fractured, prejudiced society like the first-
century world, God's eternal purpose demonstrated that his peace
was possible among people and that there was hope for humanity
to live in unity. The church in America today and the world can be
the hope of heaven once again.

God's eternal purpose and manifold wisdom flow out of what
the apostle called the "mystery of Christ" (Ephesians 3:4). It is indisputable that Paul saw the gospel of Jesus Christ as the means by
which God kept his promise to Abraham (see Romans 15:8–21). It is
indisputable as well that Paul preached a gospel that reconciled and
unified Jews and Gentiles (see Ephesians 2:1–22; 3:6–7). Let's review
his words again to drive this gospel reality into our DNA:

This mystery is that the Gentiles are fellow heirs, members of the
same body, and partakers of the promise in Christ Jesus through
the gospel.

> Of this gospel I was made a minister according to the gift of God's grace, which was given me by the working of his power. To me, though I am the very least of all the saints, this grace was given, to preach to the Gentiles the unsearchable riches of Christ, and to bring to light for everyone what is the plan of the mystery hidden for ages in God who created all things. (Ephesians 3:6–9)

The promise is the one God made to Abraham that he would give Abraham a big, multiethnic family (see Genesis 12:1–3).

> Remember that you were at that time separated from Christ, alienated from the commonwealth of Israel and strangers to the covenants of promise, having no hope and without God in the world. But now in Christ Jesus you who once were far off have been brought near by the blood of Christ. (Ephesians 2:12–13)

> Know then that it is those of faith who are the sons of Abraham. And the Scripture, foreseeing that God would justify the Gentiles by faith, preached the gospel beforehand to Abraham, saying, "In you shall all the nations be blessed." So then, those who are of faith are blessed along with Abraham, the man of faith. . . .

> So that in Christ Jesus the blessing of Abraham might come to the Gentiles, so that we might receive the promised Spirit through faith. (Galatians 3:7–9, 14)

I'm taking time to review these texts because I want you to see it is indisputable that the apostle started multiethnic local churches because he joined God in fulfilling the covenant with Abraham and local Jewish-Gentile churches were a sign of God's faithfulness. These local churches were birthed out of the blood of Jesus, revealing the mystery of Christ, the manifold wisdom of God—God's eternal purpose.

I HAVE TWO QUESTIONS

If this is true—and it is—why is there so little preaching, teaching, and writing about it? In America, the bestselling Christian books are self-help books. It appears we care more about accomplishing the American Dream than partnering with Jesus to accomplish his Father's dream (see Ephesians 3:6–13). And even among so-called theologians, there is little mention of God's multiethnic church tied to God's promises to Abraham.

If this is true—and it is—why has planting and continuing homogeneous churches, not just in America but the world, become the norm?

If this is true—and it is—I'm calling for a biblical, Christ-centered, missional church-planting and church-building resurgence of God's eternal purpose: the mystery of Christ in America and the world. I'm calling for it because it is the very heartbeat of God himself.

I'm calling for, and I believe God is calling for, pastors, elders, church leaders, and congregations to fulfill their divine birth in becoming ambassadors of gospel-shaped reconciliation, so they join God in keeping his covenant to Abraham. Paul was a multiethnic local church planter; his concern was proclaiming the gospel so the

Holy Spirit could unite people in Christ so they could be united in a Jewish-Gentile congregation in order to display the mystery of Christ as a foretaste of the eternal church.

In America, we must break our addiction to conversion stats and viewing church as a nightclub for Jesus. We must start developing hearts for God's purpose for his church. Only deep discipleship can withstand the furnace and spiritual warfare of planting and building local multiethnic churches.

HE GAVE HIS LIFE TESTIFYING TO THE GOSPEL OF THE GRACE OF GOD

As evangelicals, we love to quote Paul's word from Acts 20:24: "But I do not account my life of any value nor as precious to myself, if only I may finish my course and the ministry that I received from the Lord Jesus, to testify to the gospel of the grace of God." Now let's look at the preceding verses:

> Now from Miletus he sent to Ephesus and called the elders of the church to come to him. And when they came to him, he said to them:
>
> "You yourselves know how I lived among you the whole time from the first day that I set foot in Asia, serving the Lord with all humility and with tears and with trials that happened to me through the plots of the Jews; how I did not shrink from declaring to you anything that was profitable, and teaching you in public and from house to house, testifying both to Jews and to Greeks

of repentance toward God and of faith in our Lord Jesus Christ."
(Acts 20:17–21)

Luke reported that Paul said this in Miletus, which is thirty miles south of Ephesus, where the apostle had planted and built multiethnic house churches. He asked the elders of the Ephesian churches to come and say good-bye to him as he prepared to go to Jerusalem. Notice what he said in the passage above: "I did not shrink from . . . testifying both to *Jews* and to *Greeks* of repentance toward God and of faith in our Lord Jesus Christ" (emphasis added). Multiethnic church planting is how Paul served the Lord with all humility, tears, trials, and plots on his life. Woe to us as pastors, elders, church leaders, and congregations that continue to reduce, truncate, or minimize the gospel of God's grace.

I write these words with much fear—fear of being dismissed by the establishment, fear of rejection by other pastors, fear of being rejected by the status quo—but my love for God and his gospel of grace overrides my fear and moves me to join Paul in saying, "Therefore I testify to you this day that I am innocent of the blood of all, for I did not shrink from declaring to you the whole counsel of God" (Acts 20:26–27). Evidently, for Paul, the whole counsel of God made much of the Lord Jesus and his gospel of grace that birthed multiethnic local churches.

Well, pastors and church leaders, what are you going to do? Are you going to become a leader captivated by God's vision of gospel-racial reconciliation and racial justice who leads a community of disciples who are trophies of God's victory and a foretaste of the world to come? Or will you continue in a colorless display of a reduced gospel that reduces God's effectiveness on earth?

In an increasingly skeptical, cynical, post-Christian America, people are looking for something beautiful. They are looking beyond the status quo. In America, we've proven we can grow big homogeneous churches, but we haven't proved we can show America how love, reconciliation, and unity look. There are glimmers of this beauty, but not enough. The bride of Christ is called to be beautiful. And *her* beauty, which is the mystery of Christ, is to be displayed in high definition when a mosaic of multicolored, multiclass, multigenerational people learn to love each other as God so loved them. That's what America and the world need.

WHEN THE HUSBAND RETURNS FOR HIS BRIDE

For a reason to be found in the boundlessness of God's love and wisdom, he decided to take me—an unchurched stutterer—and give me a gift to lead and teach the gospel of grace. As a result of God's eternal purpose, he's given me some wonderful opportunities to preach the gospel all over the world. As much as I love preaching and seeing Jesus made much of, I hurt every time I leave home. Before I hit the door, I'm already thinking about returning to see my children. But I'm even more excited to return and see my bride. Vicki has been my best friend and source of encouragement since I was eighteen years old. I love her and there is nothing I would not do for her. With each passing year, I understand Ephesians 5:25 more and more: "Husbands, love your wives, as Christ loved the church and gave himself up for her."

I love Vicki. Love is a demonstration of one's affections to another; therefore, when I am away from her, I long to return to her. Jesus, with a love that is infinitely perfect, longs to return for his bride, the church. Jesus is returning to earth for his beautiful, multicolored bride. Christ longs to see *her* face because in looking at the beauty of *her* face, the mystery of Christ is revealed (see Ephesians 3:6). And we know that his bride is beautiful because his grace "cleansed her by the washing of water with the word, so that he might present the church to himself in splendor, without spot or wrinkle or any such thing, that she might be holy and without blemish" (Ephesians 5:26–27).

END TIME DEBATES

Jesus is returning, and I have no idea when. Actually no one knows but the Father (see Mark 13:32). I'm more concerned about what his bride is supposed to be doing until he returns. The scope of this book is not an attempt to untangle the various webs of end-times scenarios but to encourage and challenge the church to realize God's eternal purpose and to be a foretaste of what the new heaven and new earth will be like. When Jesus returns within God's new creation, this will happen:[2]

- God will remake heaven and earth completely, affirming the goodness of the original creation and ending its corruption and finality (see Isaiah 65:17; 66:22; Romans 8:18–25; Revelation 21:1).

- Jesus will reappear and usher in the age to come (see Matthew 12:32; Mark 10:30; Luke 18:30; Colossians 3:4; 1 John 3:2).

- When Jesus appears, those Christians who are still alive will be changed, transformed, so that their mortal bodies will become incorruptible, like Christ's glorified, resurrected body (Luke 15:22–23; 50–54; 1 Corinthians 15:22–23; Philippians 3:20–21; Colossians 3:4; 1 Thessalonians 4:16–17; 1 John 3:2).

- When Jesus appears, the resurrection will occur. All who have died in Christ will rise again from the dead and take on a body of immortality, just like Jesus' glorified, resurrected body (Luke 15:22–23; 50–54; 1 Corinthians 15:22–23; Philippians 3:20–21; Colossians 3:4; 1 Thessalonians 4:16–17; 1 John 3:2).

- The day the resurrection occurs is also called "the last day" (or "the latter day") and "the day of the Lord," and it will come unexpectedly (Job 19:25–26 KJV; Joel 2:1–3; Amos 5:18–20; Zechariah 14:1–4; John 6:39–44, 54; 11:24; 12:48; 2 Corinthians 1:13–14; Philippians 1:6; 1 Thessalonians 5:2; 2 Thessalonians 2:2 NIV; 2 Peter 3:8–12.)

- The coming of Christ in glory, which will usher forth the resurrected, glorified bodies of the redeemed, is the Christian's hope (Romans 5:2; Acts 23:6; 1 Corinthians 15:22; Colossians 1:27; Titus 2:13; 1 Peter 1:13; 5:1, 4).

- The resurrection will occur on the "day of redemption"

when our bodies will be redeemed as well as the earth itself (Ephesians 4:30; Luke 21:28; Romans 8:18–24).

- Both the just and the unjust will rise again. And Jesus will judge both. The just in Christ will spend eternity in the new heaven and new earth, and the unjust will spend eternity separated from God (Daniel 12:1–3; John 5:28–29; Acts 24:15; Romans 14:10; 1 Corinthians 4:5; 2 Timothy 4:1–8; 2 Corinthians 5:10).

- The Lord will be revealed from heaven and return with thousands of his holy ones to judge the earth and show himself to be king over all (1 Thessalonians 1:7–10; 3:13; 4:15; 2 Thessalonians 2:8; 1 Timothy 6:14–15; Jude 14–15; Revelation 19–22).

Jesus is returning, and when he does, wonderful, mind-blowing things will happen. The garden that was lost will be transformed into a city of the redeemed, and God will dwell with his multi-ethnic people. In the new heavens and new earth there will not be segregation.

But until that day, we, the bride of Christ, must be ready for his return. Our readiness will serve as a witness to those trapped in darkness that the God of light and love is a husband who seeks their hand in marriage.

As Jesus' bride, who reveals the mystery of Christ, how do we prepare for his return? How do we act as a display and foretaste of Jesus' victory? I want to introduce you to one of the greatest leaders in the world, not just the Christian world: Célestin Musekura.

THE TEARS OF RWANDA

"The Tutsi-led Rwandan Patriotic Front (RPF) invaded its home country of Rwanda in October 1990. This incident instigated the tribal war between the Tutsi minority and the Hutu-led government and its Rwandan Armed Forces."[3] The inconceivable happened just four years later: over a period of just one hundred days, nearly one million people were massacred in Rwanda's genocide.

Célestin Musekura knows the horror of Rwanda's genocide all too well; in the midst of this unspeakable horror, members of his family and members of the congregation he pastored were killed.[4] In *Forgiven as We've Been Forgiven*, Célestin wrote: "I found pastors and church leaders who had survived the killings and who were mourning the loss of their wives, children, colleagues and church members. Most of these pastors, priests and church leaders were asking, 'Does God care ab67out us? Is God really all-powerful? Where was God when my wife and children were being chopped into pieces? Are we in the days of great tribulation?'"[5]

As a result of the horror that Célestin's country experienced, the Lord Jesus called him to preach reconciliation in Rwanda and to plant multiethnic churches that were made of Hutus and Tutsis. His gospel vision was to have congregations made of enemies who killed each other's families to now be one in Christ. His gospel vision was to see people who had broken each other into bloody pieces now break communion bread and drink the forgiving, reconciling blood of Jesus. God called him to display how the mystery of Christ could bring healing to a nation ripped apart by ethnic hatred and murder.

Célestin knew that the apostle Paul's words in Ephesians 2:14–16 (NLT) had the power to resurrect a nation from the dead:

> For Christ himself has brought peace to us. He united Jews and Gentiles into one people when, in his own body on the cross, he broke down the wall of hostility that separated us. He did this by ending the system of law with its commandments and regulations. He made peace between Jews and Gentiles by creating in himself one new people from the two groups. Together as one body, Christ reconciled both groups to God by means of his death on the cross, and our hostility toward each other was put to death.

Célestin knew that only the Prince of Peace could bring peace to Hutus and Tutsis who hated each other. Célestin knew that only Jesus could transform the two tribes into a new tribe called the church. Célestin knew that only Jesus through his death on the cross could kill the ethnic hatred between the Hutus and Tutsis. Célestin knew that only the gospel of Jesus Christ and his amazing grace could teach and empower enemies to love one another.

As a result of this gospel conviction, Célestin launched the African Leadership and Reconciliation Ministries (ALARM). Célestin has a PhD in theological studies from Dallas Theological Seminary. He's done extensive research on contemporary models of forgiveness, specializing in communal forgiveness, servant leadership, and justice administration. His passion is to train church leaders in Rwanda to understand that the gospel and our new ethnicity in Christ "trumps the obligations of tribe."[6]

Célestin is a disciple shaped by the gospel of God.

EXPORTING A THEOLOGY OF SEGREGATION

About his home continent of Africa, Célestin wrote: "Today, even in major cities that are multi-ethnic and multi-cultural, we still have single-ethnicity congregations using tribal language for their Sunday services. . . . This is not unlike the situation in many historically white and black churches in North America."

Tribalism and ethnic hostility already existed in Africa, and then "Christian missionaries from the West" came to Africa and preached a reduced gospel that fostered tribalism and hostility by building monoethnic and tribal congregations. Célestin wrote: "The majority of Christians did not understand where their loyalty was. Many felt as though they were Hutu or Tutsi first, then Christian second."[7] Célestin said that Western missionaries emphasized getting conversions rather than making disciples. They preached about how to go to heaven rather than the gospel of grace that produces disciples who practice reconciliation, forgiveness, and unity. Therefore, the Hutus and Tutsis remained loyal to their tribal identity, and when the war broke out, they cut each other apart with hatchets.

Christian history is full of examples of believers who did not apply God's message of unity and reconciliation equally. Jonathan Edwards, the greatest theologian America has ever produced, owned slaves. And many states had laws that prevented Blacks from pursuing education alongside White students. "Southern Baptist

Theological Seminary in Louisville, Kentucky, began teaching black students on its campus in 1942 in a 'Negro Extension Department.' Initially, they received instruction from professors and graduate students in vacant faculty offices since a Kentucky law prohibited educational institutions from teaching both white and African American students as pupils."[8]

In 1787, the African Methodist Episcopal Church was started by two Black men, Richard Allen and Absalom Jones, because of the racist practices of St. George Methodist Episcopal Church in Philadelphia. Reconciliation did not place until 2009! On October 25, 2009, The Great Gathering took place at St. George's in which the community of Mother Bethel AME and St. George's congregations gathered for Sunday worship at St. George's for the first time since the historic walkout two centuries earlier.[9] Sadly, it was this theology of segregation that was exported to Africa.

As Célestin preached reconciliation, fellow Hutus said he was betraying his people by asking them to repent and seek forgiveness. The Tutsis hated him because he confronted them with the gospel message of forgiveness and restoration. As a result, Célestin was beaten three times in refugee camps and tortured for three and half hours at a police brigade.[10]

Just as American Christians did not know, our Rwandan brothers and sisters did not know that Jesus made Hutus and Tutsis into "one new man," into a new tribe (see Ephesians 2:15). This is why the apostle Paul said there is neither Jew nor Greek, because those who place their trust in Christ are one in Christ. They are a blood-bought, blood-washed, blood-transformed ethnicity called the children of Abraham (see Galatians 3:28–29). My primary identity is a child of God who happens to be Black. My blackness and cultural upbringing are not my primary identity, but being in Christ is.

As Paul said, we are baptized and clothed in Christ (see Galatians 3:27). We have a new family of origin that now has our allegiance. We now owe loyalty to the Father of the Lord Jesus. We are birthed into the tribe of Jesus. And this tribe is a brotherhood and sisterhood of multiethnic people. If only we'd let the gospel truth of this sink into our DNA.

ON A SUNDAY MORNING

On a Sunday morning in 1997, uniformed men with clubs, swords, guns, and grenades invaded a village and killed seventy people. Among those murdered were Célestin's father, other family members, and friends.[11] In a raw moment of hurt and anger that I can't imagine, Célestin wanted revenge! And the God of grace challenged him to practice the reconciliation and forgiveness he had been preaching to others. Célestin reported what God told him:

> You have been teaching others about repentance and forgiveness. You do well in instructing others and leading others toward forgiveness. It is now your turn to forgive those who killed your relatives without asking where I was. It is your turn to forgive those who brutally murdered your loved ones, even before you know their names. It is up to you to make a choice: either forgive and let me take care of the rest or fail to forgive and give up your freedom, joy and peace. You can either choose to be a hypocrite who teaches what he does not practice, or you can be

the wounded healer who gives the healing gift of forgiveness to the undeserving.[12]

This is what God's people should be doing before Jesus returns. This is what being a beautiful bride looks like. Love and forgiveness to the underserving is a witness to Jesus' victory over sin, death, and evil. This is gospel-shaped leadership.

The same gospel that empowers Célestin Musekura and that is rebuilding Rwanda is the same gospel that can transform the church in America and throughout the world. This is what the bride of Christ should be about until our husband returns.

BEAUTIFUL BRIDE

In Colossi, the apostle Paul planted multiethnic churches (see Colossians 1:27; 3:11). These churches had Jews and a variety of Gentiles who had past hostilities with one another. Yet in the midst of this ethnocentrism, racism, and classism, God the Holy Spirit guided Paul to write these words to bless the Colossian churches: "Here there is not Greek and Jew, circumcised and uncircumcised, barbarian, Scythian, slave, free; but Christ is all, and in all" (3:11).

As their spiritual father, Paul pleaded with the Colossian church to exchange their old identities for Jesus' new identity. He wanted them to exchange their former allegiances to their previous ethnicities and tribes and to take hold of the gospel reality that they are a new ethnicity and new tribe in Christ called the mystery of Christ.

Then Paul described what a beautiful multiethnic local church looks like:

> Put on then, as God's chosen ones, holy and beloved, compassionate hearts, kindness, humility, meekness, and patience, bearing with one another and, if one has a complaint against another, forgiving each other; as the Lord has forgiven you, so you also must forgive. And above all these put on love, which binds everything together in perfect harmony. And let the peace of Christ rule in your hearts, to which indeed you were called in one body. And be thankful. Let the word of Christ dwell in you richly, teaching and admonishing one another in all wisdom, singing psalms and hymns and spiritual songs, with thankfulness in your hearts to God. And whatever you do, in word or deed, do everything in the name of the Lord Jesus, giving thanks to God the Father through him. (Colossians 3:12–17)

Until our husband, the Lord Jesus, returns, we are to progressively grow in our beautiful relationships with one another. According to Paul, beauty looks like love, compassion, kindness, humility, meekness, and patience (see Colossians 3:12–13). Can you imagine a world filled with people who exhibit these characteristics? Isn't that beautiful? In an ugly world, beauty like this is simply irresistible. Local churches of love and beauty become a haven of hope to a hopeless world. The body of Christ becomes the corporate expression of Jesus to our world.

The power for this beautiful community is found in union life with Jesus. We can't flourish or be beautiful on our own. Only Jesus can be beautiful *in us* and *through us* as we live by faith in him. In

Christ, we are chosen, holy, and beloved. All these identities belong to Jesus. And by our union life in Jesus, his chosenness, his holiness, and his belovedness are ours as gifts and the sources of power to flourish. Our local churches can become communities of love, reconciliation, unity, and flourishing because of Christ in us, the hope of glory.

STUDY QUESTIONS, REFLECTIONS, AND PRAYER

1. What do I mean by *"Gospel-shaped ministry leaders begin with the end in mind"*?
   a. What does the end look like according to Revelation 5:9–12?
   b. How does this affect the way you view leadership today?
3. Read Acts 20:17–20, 24. Since Paul counted his life as nothing for the sake of the gospel, who was he committed to reaching with the gospel to produce ethnically diverse local churches?
4. Discuss the story of Célestin Musekura. Share the stories of other Christians you may know who are bringing reconciliation to difficult situations.
5. What about Dr. Musekura's commitment to the gospel, reconciliation, and multiethnic church planting inspires you? What in his story challenges you?
6. Discuss the following statement: *"Disciples shaped by the gospel want to create churches that go beyond saving souls to building communities that save the world."*

PRAYER

Father, I pray for all those who have read this book that these words will be an ever-present gospel reality in their lives and churches:

The power for this beautiful community is found in union life with Jesus. We can't flourish or be beautiful on our own. Only Jesus can be beautiful *in us* and *through us* as we live by faith in him. In Christ, we are chosen, holy, and beloved. All these identities belong to Jesus. And by our union life in Jesus, his chosenness, his holiness, and his belovedness are ours as gifts and the sources of power to flourish. Our local churches can become communities of love, reconciliation, unity, and flourishing because of Christ in us, the hope of glory.

In Jesus' name, amen.

CONCLUSION

ARE YOU IN?

Thank you for reading this book. In writing it, I've learned so much. I'm not the same man who started this book. Jesus has transformed me personally and has deepened my passion for his eternal purpose: the church. More than ever, I believe that the planting and building of multiethnic local churches throughout America and the world is a sign of God's faithfulness to the covenant promise he made with Abraham. And that promise was to give Abraham a big, blessed multiethnic family that gathers locally throughout the earth.

In light of this biblical conviction, let's look at the end of Paul's letter to the Romans. My doctoral advisor and friend, Scot McKnight said, "Derwin, if you want to know why Paul wrote a letter, read the end of the letter first." So to find out why Paul wrote to the Christians in Rome, let's look at the last chapter:

> For I tell you that Christ became a servant to the circumcised to show God's truthfulness, in order to confirm the promises given

215

to the patriarchs, and in order that the Gentiles might glorify
God for his mercy. As it is written,

> "Therefore I will praise you among the Gentiles,
> and sing to your name."

And again it is said,

> "Rejoice, O Gentiles, with his people."

And again,

> "Praise the Lord, all you Gentiles,
> and let all the peoples extol him."

And again Isaiah says,

> "The root of Jesse will come,
> even he who arises to rule the Gentiles;
> in him will the Gentiles hope."

May the God of hope fill you with all joy and peace in believing, so that by the power of the Holy Spirit you may abound in
hope." (Romans 15:8–13)

The apostle said "that Christ became a servant to the circumcised to show God's truthfulness, in order to confirm the promises
given to the patriarchs, and in order that the Gentiles might glorify

God for his mercy" (15:8). There it is: Jesus, the Messiah himself, through his sinless life, substitutionary atoning death on the cross, resurrection, and ascension to the right hand of the Father, is God's faithfulness to keep his covenant promise made with Abraham to give him a big, beautiful multiethnic family. Local multiethnic churches are the fulfillment of this God's faithfulness. This is the gospel Paul preached: "Of this gospel I was made a minister according to the gift of God's grace, which was given me by the working of his power" (Ephesians 3:7). All of Jesus' actions were to realize this gospel reality: "This was according to the eternal purpose that he has *realized* in Christ Jesus our Lord, in whom we have boldness and access with confidence through our faith in him" (Ephesians 3:11–12, emphasis added).

In America and the rest of the world today, we don't think about the division as just between Jew and Gentile anymore, but we see strife between people everywhere. Jesus rescued us with his blood and through his resurrection to point to a greater, richer, more beautiful reality. This reality is that God himself would indwell a multiethnic people who now function as God's temple (see Ephesians 2:21–22). This new multicolored temple was created to display to the world that God was faithful in keeping his covenant promise to Abraham.

May we be found faithful to partner with God in accomplishing this gospel reality. May we be able to say with the apostle Paul:

In Christ Jesus, then, I have reason to be proud of my work for God. For I will not venture to speak of anything except what Christ has accomplished through me to bring the Gentiles to

obedience—by word and deed, by the power of signs and won-
ders, by the power of the Spirit of God—so that from Jerusalem
and all the way around to Illyrium I have fulfilled the ministry
of the gospel of Christ; and thus I make it my ambition to preach
the gospel, not where Christ has already been named, lest I build
on someone else's foundation, but as it is written,

> "Those who have never been told of him will see,
> and those who have never heard will understand."
> (Romans 15:17–21)

The world needs ministry leaders who are captured by the gospel vison of reconciliation. Will you be one?

DEVELOP A STRATEGY

1. Take time to review your notes and conversations. Now,
   develop a strategy using what you've learned to plant a multiethnic church or to transition a homogeneous church into a
   multiethnic church.
2. If you are interested in joining me and the Transformation
   Church leadership team for a roundtable equipping session,
   please contact me at pastorderwin@transformationchurch.tc.

ACKNOWLEDGMENTS

Those who make a difference are those who understand, value, and develop partnerships. This book is the outworking of partnerships. This book would not be possible without my wife, Vicki, and my children, Presley and Jeremiah. The way my family loves and calls me to fulfill my purpose in Christ is fuel to my soul.

The Transformation staff and Transformer congregation have been the classroom for the gospel-shaped theology and practices of this book. This book was birthed in the midst of blood, sweat, tears, prayer, funerals, and weddings. But above all, this book is the lovechild of trusting Jesus to create a gospel-drenched, multiethnic church that acts as a means of love, grace, and reconciliation in our racially divided world.

I am grateful for Chris McGinn, my extra set of editorial eyes. I am thankful for my friend Lysa Terkeurst; her inspiration and "muscle" behind this project was epic. I am thankful for the Thomas Nelson team and their belief in the transformative power of this book.

Ultimately, I am indebted to the Father, who is good. The Son, who is gracious. And the Holy Spirit, who is present and powerful.

Finally, I want to thank you, the reader. In these pages, you will be called to the epic work of building Jesus-focused, gospel-shaped, multiethnic local churches. It will cost you everything. But what Jesus restores to you and creates through you will be worth it.

NOTES

Chapter 1: Gospel-Shaped Leadership

1. Valerie Strauss, "For First Time, Minority Students Expected to Be Majority in U.S. Public Schools This Fall," *Washington Post*, August 21, 2014, http://www.washingtonpost.com/blogs/answer -sheet/wp/2014/08/21/for-first-time-minority-students-expected-to -be-majority-in-u-s-public-schools-this-fall.
2. Paul Taylor, "The Next America," *Pew Research*, April 10, 2014, http://www.pewresearch.org/next-america/#The-New-Us.
3. Taylor, "Next America."
4. Mark Lopez, quoted in Taylor, "Next America."
5. Kim Lachance Shadrow, "Closer to a Comeback? BlackBerry Says It's Ready to Hire Again," *Entrepreneur*, August 6, 2014, http://www .entrepreneur.com/article/236254.
6. Cathy Lynn Grossman, "Sunday Is Still the Most Segregated Day of the Week," America: The Jesuit Review, January 16, 2015, https:// www.americamagazine.org/content/all-things/sunday-still-most -segregated-day-week.
7. Cathy Lynn Grossman, "Sunday Is Still the Most Segregated Day of the Week."
8. Grossman.
9. David A. DeSilva, *Transformation* (Bellington: Lexham, 2014), 83.
10. Cited in Mark DeYmaz, *HUP: Should Pastors Accept or Reject the Homogeneous Unit Principle?* (Dallas: Leadership Network, 2012), 8.

11. Bird, *Evangelical Theology*, 557.

12. Cited in Tierney Sneed, "Ferguson Report Prompts Resignations, Court Takeover," *U.S. News & World Report*, March 11, 2015, https://www.usnews.com/news/articles/2015/03/11/doj -ferguson-report-prompts-resignations-court-takeover.

13. Scot McKnight was my doctoral advisor. He said this to me in conversation and gave me permission to share it in this book.

14. See Ken Hutcherson's testimony online at "Ken Hutcherson: White Chair Film - I Am Second®," 4:58, YouTube video published by I Am Second, February 4, 2010, https://www.youtube.com /watch?v=IzN7kLVVzwk. Do yourself a favor and watch it.

15. Michael F. Bird, *Evangelical Theology: A Biblical and Systematic Introduction* (Grand Rapids: Zondervan, 2013), 559.

16. N. T. Wright, *Paul and the Faithfulness of God* (Minneapolis: Fortress Press, 2013), 1487. Used by permission.

17. Michael Emerson, cited in DeYmaz, *HUP*, 11.

18. Rodney Stark, *The Rise of Christianity: A Sociologist Reconsiders History* (Princeton, NJ: Princeton University Press, 1996), 213.

19. Kevin D. Dougherty, Mark Chaves, and Michael O. Emerson, "Racial Diversity in U.S. Congregations, 1998–2019," *Journal for the Scientific Study of Religion*, October 16, 2020, 8–9, https://doi.org /10.1111/jssr.12681.

20. Dougherty, Chaves, and Emerson, "Racial Diversity," 8–9.

21. Michael O. Emerson, The HD Leader Roundtable, November 9–10, 2020, https://www.derwinlgray.com/hd-roundtable-open; Emerson, email message to author, October 8, 2020.

22. Michael O. Emerson, email message to author, October 8, 2020.

23. Dougherty, Chaves, and Emerson, "Racial Diversity," 10.

24. Dougherty, Chaves, and Emerson, 10.

25. Steven Henderson, "Why Are People of Color Leaving White Evangelical Churches?," *Detroit Today*, July 3, 2018, https://wdet .org/posts/2018/07/03/86978-why-are-people-of-color-leaving -white-evangelical-churches/.

26. Dougherty, Chaves, and Emerson, "Racial Diversity," 10.

27. Dougherty, Chaves, and Emerson, "Racial Diversity," 10.

28. Dougherty, Chaves, and Emerson, 9–10.

CHAPTER 2: SEEING LIFE FOR THE FIRST TIME

1. Samuel Benson, "BYU Football: The All-Time Dream Team,"
   Bleacher Report, August 15, 2012, http://bleacherreport.com
   /articles/1297932-byu-football-the-all-time-dream-team/page/8.

2. Christopher J. H. Wright, *The Mission of God: Unlocking the Bible's
   Grand Narrative* (Downers Grove, IL: IVP Academic, 2006), 191.

3. See "2013 Outreach 100 Fastest-Growing Churches in America,"
   Outreach Magazine, http://www.outreachmagazine.com/2013
   -outreach-100-fastest-growing-churches-america.html.

CHAPTER 3: SEEING SALVATION THROUGH THE LENS OF UPWARD, INWARD, OUTWARD

1. Upward, Inward, Outward is a concept I received from Ken Boa.
   His book *Conformed to His Image: Biblical and Practical Approaches
   to Spiritual Formation* (Grand Rapids: Zondervan, 2001) has greatly
   shaped my theology and Christian living.

2. Soong-Chan Rah, *The Next Evangelicalism: Releasing the Church
   from Western Cultural Captivity* (Downers Grove, IL: InterVarsity
   Press, 2009), 85.

3. My friend David Anderson coined this phrase in his book *Gracism:
   The Art of Inclusion* (Downers Grove, IL: InterVarsity Press, 2007).

4. Roswell D. Hitchcock, "Entry for 'Damascus,'" *An Interpreting
   Dictionary of Scripture Proper Names* (New York, 1869), cited at
   "Damascus," *Bible Study Tools*, http://www.biblestudytools.com/
   dictionary/damascus.

5. N. T. Wright, *Paul and the Faithfulness of God* (Minneapolis:
   Fortress Press, 2013), 1506. Used by permission.

6. See Revelation 5:9–12.

7. William Barclay, ed., *The Letters to the Galatians and Ephesians*
   (Philadelphia: Westminster Press, 1976), 107.

8. Quoted in Barclay, *Letters to the Galatians and Ephesians*, 113.

9. Wright, *Paul and the Faithfulness of God*, 1494. Used by permission.

10. Wright, 1494.

11. Curtiss Paul DeYoung, et al., *United by Faith: The Multiracial Congregation as an Answer to the Problem of Race* (New York: Oxford University Press, 2003), 54–55.

12. DeYoung, et al., *United by Faith*, 57.

13. Quoted in DeYoung et al., 58.

14. DeYoung et al., 59.

15. Rah, *Next Evangelicalism*, 83.

16. Rah, 29.

17. Mark DeYmaz, *Building a Healthy Multiethnic Church* (San Francisco: Jossey-Bass, 2007), 23–24.

CHAPTER 4: SEEING CHRIST JESUS AND GOD'S ETERNAL PLAN

1. See Hebrews 9:14. The Holy Spirit is coequal and coeternal with the Father and the Son.

2. J. Daniel Hays, *From Every People and Nation: A Biblical Theology of Race* (Downers Grove, IL: InterVarsity Press, 2003), 188.

3. For a more in-depth exploration of this gorgeous story, see my book *Limitless Life: You Are More Than Your Past When God Holds Your Future* (Nashville: Thomas Nelson, 2013).

4. Quoted in Mark DeYmaz, *Leading a Healthy Multiethnic Church* (Grand Rapids: Zondervan, 2010), 12–13.

5. Christopher J. H. Wright, *The Mission of God: Unlocking the Bible's Grand Narrative* (Downers Grove, IL: InterVarsity Press, 2006), 191.

6. Rodney Stark, *The Rise of Christianity: A Sociologist Reconsiders History* (Princeton: Princeton University Press, 1996), 157.

7. See Mark DeYmaz, "Ethnic Blends: Growing Healthy, Multiethnic Churches," *Facts and Trends*, October 9, 2014, http://factsandtrends.net/2014/10/09/ethnic-blends-growing-healthy-multiethnic-churches/#.VD_vfPldWSo.

Chapter 5: Seeing Missionally and Reconciliationally

1. Mark Chaves and Shawna L. Anderson, "Changing American Congregations: Findings from the Third Wave of the National Congregations Study," *Journal for the Scientific Study of Religion* 53, no. 4 (December 2014): 676–86, http://onlinelibrary.wiley.com/doi/10.1111/.jssr.12151/abstract.

2. Helen Lee, "Asian Americans: Silent No More," *Christianity Today*, October 6, 2014, 39–47, https://www.christianitytoday.com/ct/2014/october/asian-american-christians-silent-no-more.html.

3. Lee, "Asian Americans," 39.

4. Greg Toppo and Paul Overberg, "Second Immigration Wave Lifts Diversity to Record High," *USA Today*, October 20, 2014, http://www.usatoday.com/longform/news/nation/2014/10/20/diversity-race-ethnicity-change-100-years/16211133.

5. Philip Jenkins, *The Next Christendom: The Coming of Global Christianity* (New York: Oxford University Press, 2011), xi.

6. Efrem Smith, conversation with the author, October 20, 2014. Used with permission.

7. Efrem Smith, *The Post-Black and Post-White Church: Becoming the Beloved Community in a Multi-Ethnic World* (San Francisco: Jossey-Bass, 2012), 2.

8. Ryan sent his thoughts in an email on November 20, 2014. Used with permission.

9. George R. Hunsberger, *Missional Church: A Vision for the Sending of the Church in North America* (Grand Rapids: Eerdmans, 1998), 101.

10. J. D. Barry et al., s.v. "John 4:9," *Faithlife Study Bible* (Bellingham, WA: Logos Bible Software, 2012).

11. J. Daniel Hays, *From Every People and Nation: A Biblical Theology of Race* (Downers Grove, IL: InterVarsity Press, 2003), 166.

12. Rebecca Barnes and Lindy Lowry, "7 Startling Facts: An Up Close Look at Church Attendance in America," *Church Leaders*, 2014, http://www.churchleaders.com/pastors/pastor-articles/139575-7-startling-facts-an-up-close-look-at-church-attendance-in-america.html/2.

13. Quoted in Cathy Lynn Grossman, "U.S. Churches Feel Beat of Change: More Diversity, More Drums," *Religion News Service*, September 11, 2014, http://www.religionnews.com/2014/09/11 /churches-change-evangelical-catholic/.

CHAPTER 6: SEEING THE BEAUTIFUL GOSPEL STORY

1. Scot McKnight, my doctoral advisor, has helped me to understand this better. See Scot McKnight, *Kingdom Conspiracy: Returning to the Radical Mission of the Local Church* (Grand Rapids: Brazos Press, 2014).
2. Frank Viola, "Rethinking the Gospel," January 26, 2012, http:// frankviola.org/2012/01/26/thegospel.
3. Daniel L. Akin, ed., *A Theology for the Church* (Nashville: B&H Academic, 2007), 688.
4. Akin, ed., *Theology for the Church*, 689.
5. The more you understand differing views, the more gracious you can be to the people who hold them. For the record, I am neither a Calvinist nor an Arminian. I am a Christian who happens to be a Paulist. Yes, I just made up that term. What does it mean? It means that I believe that Christ is the elect man who represents humanity. We are individually and corporately the elect in the Son by faith as God the Holy Spirit reveals Christ to us. Within my theological framework, this issue for me is not about God's sovereignty versus man's free will. I have learned much and appreciate both Calvinism and Arminianism; both theological frameworks have their strong and weak points. Because God is outside of time and time is within him, God in his majestic, sovereign beauty is at the end at the same moment he is at the beginning. My view of election is Christological. My primary concern with the doctrine of election is that whoever is in Christ by faith is united to him and possesses every spiritual blessing in him, which empowers them to live on earth in communities of local multiethnic congregations of unified, reconciled people to praise God's glorious grace.

6. N. T. Wright, *Paul and the Faithfulness of God* (Minneapolis: Fortress Press, 2013), 1494–95. Used by permission.

Chapter 7: Seeing the Church Through a Gospel Vision

1. Credit for this discovery goes to Brandon Robinson, a pastor in training at Transformation Church on April 23, 2015.
2. J. D. Barry et al., s.v. "1 Timothy 3:9," *Faithlife Study Bible* (Bellingham, WA: Logos Bible Software, 2012). Also see R. J. Utley, *Paul's Fourth Missionary Journey: 1 Timothy, Titus, II Timothy* (Marshall, TX: Bible Lessons International, 2000), 9:46.
3. D. A. Carson et al., *New Bible Commentary: 21st Century Edition*, 4th ed. (Downers Grove, IL: InterVarsity Press, 1994), 1234.
4. Jeanne Kim, "The World's Greatest Fears, Mapped by Country," *The Atlantic*, October 20, 2014, http://m .theatlantic.com/international/archive/2014/10 /the-worlds-greatest-fears-mapped-by-country/381678.

Chapter 8: Seeing Discipleship and Leadership Through the Gospel

1. Transformation Church, "New Here?" http://www .transformationchurch.tc/newhere/visionvalues.php.
2. We grasped the idea of community, congregation, committed, and core from Rick Warren's *The Purpose Driven Church: Growth Without Compromising Your Message and Mission* (Grand Rapids: Zondervan, 1995).
3. I came across the three C's of character, competency, and chemistry in Bill Hybels's *Courageous Leadership* (Grand Rapids: Zondervan, 2002), 81.

Chapter 9: Seeing the World to Come

1. J. W. Carter, "Ephesians 2:11–22: Unity in the Body of Christ," *American Journal of Biblical Theology*, 2011, http://www .biblicaltheology.com/eph/49_02_11.html.

2. Leonard Sweet and Frank Viola, *Jesus: A Theography* (Nashville: Thomas Nelson, 2012), 290–91.

3. L. Gregory Jones and Célestin Musekura, *Forgiving as We've Been Forgiven: Community Practices for Making Peace* (Downers Grove, IL: InterVarsity Press, 2010), 15.

4. Sweet and Viola, *Jesus*, 290–91.

5. Jones and Musekura, *Forgiving as We've Been Forgiven*, 17.

6. "Rev. Célestin Musekura, Ph.D., Founder," ALARM, https://www.alarm-inc.org/thefounder/.

7. "Rev. Célestin Musekura, ALARM.

8. David Roach, "Ethnic Participation in Convention Ministry: A Historical Perspective on the Election of Fred Luter," SBC Life, October 2012, http://www.sbclife.net/Articles/2012/10/sla5.

9. Suzy Keenan, "Service Overcomes Two Centuries of Division," United Methodists of the California-Nevada Annual Conference, October 27, 2009, http://www.cnumc.org/news/6846.

10. Keenan, "Service Overcomes Two Centuries of Division," 19.

11. Keenan, 20.

12. Keenan, 21–22.

ABOUT THE AUTHOR

Dr. Derwin L. Gray is the founding and lead pastor of Transformation Church (TC). Transformation Church is a multiethnic, multigeneration, mission-shaped community in the Charlotte, North Carolina area. Derwin and Vicki have been married for twenty-eight years and have two adult children. Derwin is the author of the bestselling book *The Good Life: What Jesus Teaches About Finding True Happiness.*